I0015175

Influence

Writing Under The Influence Of A
Millennial Emergence

*(How to Make Media Love You Influence People
and Explode Awareness About Your Innovation
Company)*

Wesley Tobin

Published By **Regina Loviusher**

Wesley Tobin

All Rights Reserved

*Influence: Writing Under The Influence Of A
Millennial Emergence (How to Make Media Love
You Influence People and Explode Awareness
About Your Innovation Company)*

ISBN   978-1-7750392-0-4

No part of this guidebook shall be reproduced in any form without permission in writing from the publisher except in the case of brief quotations embodied in critical articles or reviews.

Legal & Disclaimer

The information contained in this book is not designed to replace or take the place of any form of medicine or professional medical advice. The information in this book has been provided for educational & entertainment purposes only.

The information contained in this book has been compiled from sources deemed reliable, and it is accurate to the best of the Author's knowledge; however, the Author cannot guarantee its accuracy and validity and cannot be held liable for any errors or omissions. Changes are periodically made to this book. You must consult your doctor or get professional medical advice before using any of the suggested remedies, techniques, or information in this book.

Upon using the information contained in this book, you agree to hold harmless the Author from and against any damages, costs, and expenses, including any legal fees potentially resulting from the application of any of the information provided by this guide. This disclaimer applies to any damages or injury caused by the use and application, whether directly or indirectly, of any advice or information presented, whether for breach of contract, tort, negligence, personal injury, criminal intent, or under any other cause of action.

You agree to accept all risks of using the information presented inside this book. You need to consult a professional medical practitioner in order to ensure you are both able and healthy enough to participate in this program.

Table Of Contents

Chapter 1: Intuitive Listening

The Foundations of Intuitive Listening

Intuitive listening rests upon two pillars: interest and empathy. It's the act of simply immersing oneself within the communiqué, suspending one's non-public judgment, and feeling the emotions of the alternative character. Empathy permits one to step into the alternative's shoes, apprehend their mindset, and create an actual emotional bond.

Example: Imagine you discover yourself in a scenario in which you need to deal with a dissatisfied customer. Instead of right now reacting with the aid of the use of protecting your position or downplaying the issues they're expressing, you pick to exercise intuitive listening. In this thoughts-set, you provide your entire hobby to what the client is announcing, aiming to apprehend now not only the terms spoken but also the underlying emotions.

You reply empathetically, acknowledging the client's frustration: «I recognize that you're annoyed with this situation, and I want to guarantee you that I'm here to help you find out an appropriate answer.» This response suggests which you've taken the time to apprehend the customer's emotions, in desire to in reality providing a popular answer.

As a quit result, the purchaser feels a experience of reassurance and knowledge. They apprehend that you're not belittling their worries but as an opportunity searching for to cope with them constructively. This empathy-driven technique creates an surroundings of agree with and mutual admire. The consumer is more likely to collaborate with you to remedy the problem satisfactorily, doubtlessly strengthening your prolonged-time period enterprise agency dating.

This instance highlights how intuitive listening can rework a possible bad state of affairs into an possibility to gather accept as true with and discover at the equal time useful answers. By presenting real interest and empathy, you could surely have an effect on the path of interactions and gain favorable outcomes.

The Science of Intuitive Listening

Neuroscience studies have validated that attentive listening turns on mind regions related to empathy and social know-how[1]. Individuals who often workout intuitive listening amplify superior interpersonal abilities, improving their interactions and function an impact on.

Example: Professor Tania Singer, a researcher who led a complete study at the University of Zurich to find out the outcomes of empathy and attentive listening on human interactions. The observe aimed to recognize how those factors have to make stronger connections amongst people. The take a look at involved recruiting people who underwent brain scans for the duration of interactions in which attentive listening became recommended.

3

The reason emerge as to measure actual-time neurological changes on the same time as a person actively engaged in deep and empathetic listening. The have a examine's findings observed out charming discoveries. When individuals engaged in interactions wherein attentive listening end up gift, there has been a massive growth in interest in mind areas associated with social praise. This heightened interest shows that attentive listening stimulates the discharge of neurotransmitters and chemical substances connected to satisfaction and well-being, for this reason reinforcing emotional bonds among people. In distinctive words, this studies gives sturdy neurological validation of the high-quality impact of attentive listening on developing more potent emotional bonds between humans. The consequences of this look at illustrate how a clean exercising of attentive listening can reason biochemical modifications in the mind, strengthening the emotional connection among people worried in an interplay[2].

The Hidden Power of Intuitive Listening

Intuitive listening is going past ordinary listening. It's the functionality to apprehend the underlying feelings and motivations in the returned of terms. When you concentrate intuitively, you show which you actually care approximately the other man or woman and recognize their desires and issues.

Example: In a have a test executed through way of Dr. Emma Johnson, negotiators were carefully divided into first-rate companies. The first organization come to be told to exercising attentive listening all through their negotiations, paying close attention to verbal and nonverbal cues from their opposite numbers. In assessment, the second one enterprise became allowed to barter without this particular listening exercise. The effects of this take a look at were large and enlightening. The agency that covered attentive listening into their negotiations accomplished agreements that have been on commonplace 17% greater favorable than those of the company that did now not. This fantastic difference in effects in reality indicates how intuitive listening can surely have an effect on the direction of negotiations.

This experiment underscores the important importance of attentive listening within the context of persuasion and negotiation. It demonstrates how the functionality to understand others' desires, issues, and feelings can reason extra favorable agreements and collectively useful effects. By incorporating intuitive listening into interactions, it's viable to forge deeper connections and acquire desires efficiently.

Intuitive Listening in Everyday Life

Intuitive listening isn't confined to expert conditions. It may be implemented in private relationships, enhancing conversation and strengthening own family and friendship bonds. By providing actual hobby and showing empathy, you may create a stable area in which others sense heard and understood.

Example: Imagine you're accrued round a own family dinner desk, and your son stocks his frustration about difficulties he's going thru at college. Instead of reacting with the resource of right away supplying advice or answers, you pick out to workout intuitive listening. You broadly recognized that your son dreams location to express his feelings and worries.

Your reaction reflects this cause. You empathetically say, «I see that this is bothering you. Can you tell me what you're feeling and the way that is affecting you?» By asking this open-ended query, you display which you're sincerely interested in what he's feeling and that you're willing to pay attention without judgment or haste.

By presenting this listening vicinity, you inspire your baby to open up further. He can also furthermore start to percent in greater element what he's experiencing emotionally and the specific reasons he famous those conditions difficult. By expressing himself on this way, he feels heard, understood, and supported through manner of you, thereby strengthening your emotional bond.

In exercising, this example illustrates how intuitive listening can create an environment of believe and open communication in the own family. Rather than right now presenting solutions, you supply your son the gap he needs to precise his feelings. As a stop cease result, he's greater willing to percent his troubles and comprise you in his private disturbing situations. This method fosters a discern-toddler dating primarily based totally mostly on mutual listening, records, and useful resource.

Intuitive Listening Across Cultures

Intuitive listening is normal, however cultural nuances can have an effect on the way it's perceived. In the united states, attentive listening is valued because it creates a feel of belonging and private connection. In Europe, it's additionally favored for its capability to enhance human relationships. In Asia, it's regularly connected to understand and honor, displaying that listening is an act of deep interest.

Chapter 2: Creating Captivating Narratives

The Magic of Captivating Narratives

Captivating narratives transcend the limits of ordinary communication. They evoke feelings, have interaction the imagination, and create profound connections. When you inform a story, you invite your listeners on a adventure that transports them past mere statistics proper into a reality infused with feelings and values.

Example: Concrete Example Dove's «Real Beauty» advertising marketing advertising marketing campaign is a powerful instance of persuasive storytelling. Instead of without a doubt promoting their merchandise, Dove suggested the story of real ladies and celebrated their herbal splendor. The advertising campaign featured a chain of images and videos showcasing real, unretouched ladies proudly displaying their precise skills. The pix had been followed through excellent and provoking messages, highlighting ideas which includes self-self assurance, self-popularity, and the celebration of variety. This preference had a profound effect on the goal market. By telling real memories of real girls, Dove efficaciously created an emotional connection with customers and therefore strengthened the logo's superb picture[3].

Elements of a Captivating Narrative

A captivating narrative includes key factors: a protagonist, a venture to triumph over, a adventure, and a decision. Emotions, conflicts, and plot twists upload depth to the narrative, attractive the audience on an emotional degree.

Example: Let's preserve in thoughts the instance of Elon Musk and SpaceX. Musk created a fascinating narrative by using way of way of portraying SpaceX as a quest to triumph over location, cope with technical demanding conditions, and inspire humanity to dream big. This narrative succeeded in captivating now not only space exploration fanatics but additionally a broader target market with grand aspirations. SpaceX rocket launches are regularly decided via stay broadcasts that exhibit key moments, which incorporates the a success landing of rocket degrees on floating systems at sea. These moments assist SpaceX's narrative via demonstrating the feasibility of rocket reusability, a crucial detail of Musk's imaginative and prescient. The most excellent impact of this persuasive storytelling became the mobilization of public and economic aid. Investors were drawn to Musk's formidable vision and the promise of revolutionizing the space business enterprise. Elon Musk and SpaceX illustrate how persuasive storytelling may be used to transform a enterprise into an thrilling and galvanizing quest. Musk's narrative captured space exploration fanatics and rallied public and financial help for his audacious vision[4].

The Psychology of Narrative Influence

Captivating narratives prompt areas of the thoughts associated with emotions and social know-how. They create neurological connections that generate lasting effect. By associating your messages with narratives, you're making them memorable and imbue them with deeper this means that.

Example: A observe finished by using way of manner of researcher Paul Zak decided that narratives that evoke pleasant feelings, along with compassion, boom the release of oxytocin, a hormone associated with social bonding. Oxytocin, moreover referred to as the «experience-suitable» or «social bonding» hormone, performs a crucial characteristic in forming and strengthening interpersonal relationships. It is often related to outstanding emotions, trust, and the formation of sturdy emotional bonds. The progressed launch of oxytocin prompted by means of manner of emotional narratives enhances the experience of connection the various storyteller and the aim marketplace. By associating your messages with emotional narratives, you enhance the memorability and importance of your content cloth material, thereby developing the effectiveness of your persuasion[5].

The Art of Narrative Creation in Practice

Crafting charming narratives requires a subtle stability between emotion and common sense. Begin via the use of figuring out your target market and their emotional wishes. Then, expand a tale that embodies your key messages on the identical time as eliciting deep emotions. Use visible, kinesthetic, and sensory facts to immerse your goal marketplace in the worldwide of the tale.

Example: Imagine you're in rate of a fundraising advertising and marketing and advertising advertising marketing campaign for a charitable organization dedicated to building colleges in underprivileged areas. Instead of simply offering records and figures approximately the importance of education, you make a decision to adopt a persuasive storytelling approach to rouse deeper emotional engagement from capability donors.

For this, you pick out to inform the tale of a specific toddler. You create a shiny portrait of this toddler via way of describing their lifestyles before and after getting access to the education provided with the useful resource of your charitable organisation. You element the challenges they had to triumph over in a hard environment, highlighting the boundaries many youngsters in these areas face.

You then describe the transformation of this little one thru schooling. You narrate how they positioned the delight of getting to know, superior abilities and competencies formerly untapped, and in the end fashioned a higher destiny for themselves and others.

By using narrative elements which consist of feelings, stressful conditions, moments of pride, and achievements, you delivery capability donors into the emotional journey of this little one.

You allow them to in my opinion hook up with their story, sense their journey, and understand the profound effect of schooling on their lifestyles.

This narrative method creates a effective emotional connection amongst capability donors and the cause you suggest for. They not see just facts; they see a real man or woman with an actual story. This conjures up sympathy, empathy, and a preference to contribute to growing a difference inside the lives of youngsters like this.

In precis, thru the usage of persuasive storytelling in this fundraising marketing and advertising marketing campaign, you have got were given transformed precis information right right right into a concrete and emotionally attractive tale. You have enabled functionality donors to deeply connect to the reason and revel in recommended to accomplish that to create a first-rate effect inside the lives of underprivileged kids.

The Ethics of Persuasive Storytelling

While the appearance of charming narratives is robust, it want to be employed ethically. Narratives want to now not manipulate or lie to the target market. Instead, intention to inspire, inform, and installation real connections.

Example: When Mr. Mycoskie, the founding father of TOMS, launched his shoe logo, he didn't accept growing a mere product. He blanketed a fundamental humanitarian mission into his enterprise model. For every pair of footwear bought, a pair modified into donated to a toddler in want. This technique now not satisfactory made a large exchange in the lives of underprivileged children but moreover normal the premise of a compelling persuasive story. Mr. Mycoskie selected to inform the story of his first revel in in Argentina, in which he witnessed the heartbreaking fact of youngsters with out shoes. By sharing this 2d of discovery, he evoked deep empathy in listeners and capability customers. This personal and right tale humanized TOMS' project, transforming a simple business transaction into an possibility to make a distinction in others' lives. By sharing his non-public enjoy, Mycoskie stable an emotional connection a number of the emblem and its clients. He stirred their sensitivity in the direction of social and humanitarian issues, illustrating how every buy might also want to have a actual and tangible effect on the vicinity. This emotional connection progressed the act beyond a trifling transaction, turning each pair of shoes into a way of expressing values and resolution to a noble reason. By integrating persuasive storytelling into his industrial agency approach, Mr. Mycoskie[6] created a significant and emotional looking for experience for TOMS' clients. He tested that proper recollections can feature catalysts to encourage movement, unite a devoted community, and undoubtedly have an impact at the brand perception.

Chapter 3: The Art of Social Proof

The Discovery of Social Proof

Social evidence is the psychological phenomenon in which human beings follow others' moves, assuming those moves are suitable. It's rooted in our need for protection and social conformity. Testimonials, online reviews, and observable behaviors are sorts of social evidence which could have an effect on our picks.

Example: In this example, agree with you're faced with a choice for dinner and also you need to determine amongst neighboring eating places. One of these ingesting places is crowded with customers, occupied tables, and a active surroundings, even as the other restaurant round the corner appears masses quieter, with only a few clients gift. The concept of social proof comes into play here. You're greater inclined to pick out the crowded eating place, even if you don't understand the meals remarkable, the issuer furnished, or in case you'll discover it impossible to resist. Why? Because the presence of a huge sort of customers creates an effect of reputation and recollect. The underlying concept is that if such a number of people have selected this restaurant, there must be a first-rate cause for it, implying that the general revel in will likely be best. This tendency to gravitate closer to what's famous or commonly determined on with the useful resource of others is a concrete instance of social proof. It's a herbal response primarily based absolutely definitely on the principle that others' moves can characteristic a manual for making our non-public selections. In distinctive phrases, we use others' selections and behaviors as a form of validation for our very very own alternatives, assuming that if many human beings are doing some aspect, it's probable an outstanding element to do. In this situation, social proof performs a enormous role within the way you examine and select the restaurant for dinner. It demonstrates how others' influences, even diffused ones, can form our normal selections and alternatives.

Sources of Social Proof

Social proof can come from numerous resources: customer testimonials, expert recommendations, social media recognition, income numbers, and so on. People are much more likely to recollect the opinion of people much like them, making testimonials mainly influential.

Example: Let's keep in thoughts the instance of an e-alternate internet website. When this internet web page presentations consumer opinions along its products, it strategically leverages social proof to persuade capability customers. The superstar rankings assigned to the goods and the high-quality feedback left through way of the usage of wonderful clients create a notion of keep in mind around the gadgets in query. This exposure to awesome feedback allows reassure destiny customers, presenting tangible proof of preceding customers' pride. As a quit end result, internet site on line site visitors experience greater willing to make a purchasing for desire, essential to improved sales for the e-change net website online on line.

The Impact of Social Proof on Decisions

The effect of social evidence can be effective. People will be inclined to bear in mind the moves of the majority due to the fact the «correct» moves. This can be decided in areas ranging from product picks to emergency behaviors, wherein humans are much more likely to do so if others are doing the identical.

Example: Let's take the have a look at completed by way of manner of researcher Solomon Asch. Participants were placed in a scenario in which they needed to answer obvious questions in a collection placing. However, examine confederates were informed to intentionally offer incorrect answers. Participants have been properly conscious that the answers furnished via the confederates were wrong. Yet, notwithstanding their understanding of the reality, almost 75% of contributors selected to conform to the employer's faulty solutions as a minimum once in the path of the test. This response is a powerful example of the impact of social pressure and the selection for conformity. This phenomenon, regularly known as the «Asch impact,» illustrates how humans are willing to conform their responses and behaviors to those of the group, even if their very personal judgment suggests in any other case. Participants felt robust pressure to avoid going toward the agency, although it supposed dismissing their personal accurate evaluation. This instance highlights how social stress can exert a powerful effect on our decisions and movements, even if we understand the path concerned approximately the useful useful resource of the enterprise organisation is incorrect. It illustrates how the choice for conformity and belonging to a fixed can outweigh our man or woman judgment and actual expertise[7].

Integrating Social Proof into Strategies

Incorporating social evidence into your persuasion strategies can be notably powerful. Use purchaser testimonials, earnings figures, information, or case studies to illustrate how others have benefited out of your services or products. Highlight the superb behaviors of the majority to inspire others to act inside the same way.

Example: Crowdfunding campaigns, together with those on Kickstarter, offer a concrete instance of the strategic use of social evidence to persuade the conduct of capability individuals. When you discover those structures, you'll frequently be conscious that every mission shows the style of humans who have already backed the advertising marketing marketing campaign, on the facet of the whole amount accrued to this point. Social evidence performs a key role proper proper here. By showing the style of people who've already contributed, the platform creates a power of reputation and assist for the undertaking. This visibility underscores that others have already made the selection to make a contribution financially. This has a mental effect on potential people. The underlying concept is if such quite some human beings have selected to aid the assignment, it have to be properly definitely worth it and sincere. Visitors are extra inclined to take part themselves, as they revel in guided through the implicit validation of the group. This approach leverages our natural tendency to show to others' choices and behaviors to guide our picks. By transparently the usage of social evidence, these structures manipulate to encourage extra contributions and foster prolonged engagement with the featured duties. This example demonstrates how the notion of recognition and help can sincerely impact human beings' alternatives in a economic and participatory context.

Traps and Ethics of Social Proof

While social evidence is a effective approach, it could also be used deceptively to govern behaviors. Brands want to be obvious and ethical of their use of social evidence. The goal want to constantly be to inform and help people in making knowledgeable selections.

Example: An industrial for a weight loss product showcases testimonials from people claiming to have out of place a big quantity of weight using the product. The testimonials are observed through first-rate earlier than-and-after photos. This creates sturdy social proof of the product's effectiveness. However, upon nearer exam, it's decided that the sooner than-and-after images had been retouched to magnify the weight reduction, and the testimonials are definitely fictional. This misleading use of social proof desires to persuade clients to shop for the product primarily based totally on faux statistics. In this case, the pitfalls of social proof are obvious. By exaggerating consequences and using fictional testimonials, the organisation tries to govern customers' buying behaviors. This unethical workout erodes consumer believe and can have negative prolonged-time period outcomes for the brand. The ethics of social evidence name for that producers gift genuine and unaltered testimonials, similarly to accurate records about the outcomes completed. By appearing transparently and providing correct facts, brands can assist clients make informed alternatives and pick out products or services that certainly match their needs.

Chapter 4: The Spark of Emotional Scarcity

The Magic of Emotional Scarcity

Emotional shortage is based totally on the precept that what's unusual is precious. When an opportunity appears limited in time, call for will increase. Individuals are encouraged to behave rapid to avoid lacking out on a completely unique threat.

Example: The instance of flash profits and constrained-time offers illustrates the utility of emotional shortage as a persuasive method. In this context, corporations provide promotions, reductions, or specific offers for a confined period, as a result growing a experience of urgency among clients. This method is based at the notion that the possibility is brief and could not present itself all once more. Emotional shortage hinges at the precept of functionality losses. Consumers are advocated to behave rapid out of fear of lacking out on an appealing offer. This worry of losing a treasured opportunity can reason feelings which incorporates anxiety, satisfaction, and hastiness. As a quit give up result, customers are more likely to make a right away looking for choice to avoid regretting not taking gain of the precise provide. However, it's critical to have a look at that excessive use of this method may additionally have terrible effects on a business enterprise's credibility. If restrained-time gives are frequent and appear synthetic, clients might likely lose accept as true with and feature a look at promotions as gimmicks in vicinity of actual possibilities. This instance underscores the power of emotional scarcity in influencing buying choices. It additionally emphasizes the want for agencies to apply this method in a balanced and apparent manner, making sure that restricted-time gives are proper and certainly useful for purchasers. When used cautiously, emotional scarcity can be an powerful manner to stimulate customer movement even as strengthening the logo-consumer courting.

Perception of Exaggerated Value

Emotional shortage amplifies the perceived price of a product or possibility. The rarer some aspect appears, the more relevant it turns into. Individuals frequently feature extra significance to items or memories which might be tough to achieve.

Example: The instance of limited-model artistic endeavors or collectible devices illustrates how emotional shortage may be used to generate sturdy interest and demand among customers. In this context, works of paintings or devices are produced in a limited quantity, because of this developing inherent shortage. Buyers are inquisitive about the concept of proudly owning some thing treasured, specific, and distinct. Emotional shortage works with the useful resource of capitalizing on the symbolic and emotional fee related to possessing uncommon objects. Consumers often companion shortage with first-class, authenticity, and exclusivity. This can generate super emotions along side delight, delight, and a experience of belonging to a pick agency. Limited-model creative endeavors and collectible devices are often placed through manner of memories and contexts that decorate their place of information and rate. These tales add an extra emotional layer to the buying revel in, strengthening the relationship most of the purchaser and the coveted object. It's critical to be aware that emotional shortage also can be manipulated to create an phantasm of synthetic shortage. For instance, some traders may additionally moreover exaggerate the rarity of a product to growth call for, which can in the long run erode purchaser keep in mind. In summary, the instance of restricted-model imaginative endeavors and collectible gadgets showcases how emotional shortage may have an impact on shopping choices through developing enchantment for specific and unique gadgets. This highlights the importance of authenticity and transparency inside the use of this approach to preserve consumer bear in mind.

Creating the Perception of Scarcity

The belief of scarcity may be created in numerous techniques: through limiting availability, setting cut-off dates, or providing unique blessings. The language applied in conversation can also play a important function in eliciting the sensation of scarcity.

Example: The instance of airways the use of emotional scarcity strategies illustrates how this approach can be achieved. When an airline claims that there are simplest «some seats left» on a particular flight, they leverage the perception of scarcity to create a revel in of urgency amongst tourists to stimulate call for and inspire customers to behave quick. This tactic capitalizes on the perishable nature of the products or offerings being provided, in this situation, aircraft seats. By suggesting that the form of seats is restricted, the airline manner that the possibility to tour on a excessive high-quality date or a particular flight may additionally vanish quick. This motivates consumers to make a quick preference to avoid lacking out at the possibility. Emotional scarcity in this context is heightened thru elements which encompass tour periods, special events, or famous places. Travelers can be stimulated through the selection now not to overlook out on particular journey possibilities or to wait massive activities. However, it's crucial to phrase that this method can also elicit terrible reactions from clients if perceived as misleading. Some airlines may additionally additionally exaggerate scarcity to encourage bookings, which can erode client consider in the long run. In precis, the instance of airlines the use of emotional shortage demonstrates how this technique can impact buy selections with the resource of growing a revel in of urgency primarily based totally on the perception of confined deliver. This technique highlights the importance of transparency and integrity within the usage of this technique to preserve customer trust.

The Effect of Emotional Scarcity on Choices

The effect of emotional shortage can extensively have an impact on our alternatives. The fear of lacking out on an exceptional possibility drives individuals to proactively are trying to find what's available in confined portions. This impulse is rooted in our choice for protection and benefit.

Example: The have a look at carried out by manner of Worchel et al. Illustrates the lack effect on consumer belief and the manner it may have an impact on their evaluation and choice for products or gadgets. In this have a take a look at, humans have been furnished with containers of cookies. One of the bins contained only some cookies, growing a belief of shortage, whilst the other area contained an abundance of cookies. Participants have been asked to assess and rate their choice for the cookies in every area. The results revealed that cookies from the scarce field have been judged as more appetizing and precious in contrast to those from the ample vicinity. This locating demonstrates the dearth impact on patron perception: whilst a few aspect is perceived as unusual or in restrained quantity, it could be taken into consideration greater precious and applicable. The clarification inside the returned of this effect lies within the psychology of shortage. Humans generally tend to characteristic improved cost to devices or opportunities which can be uncommon, as they're gave the look to be more hard to collect. This notion reinforces the selection to own the ones gadgets, regardless of the truth that their real application doesn't vary from extra ample ones. In the context of purchase selection-making, this situation highlights how corporations can leverage the dearth effect to growth the perceived price of their products and virtually have an effect on purchaser alternatives. However, it's important for this method to be used ethically and transparently to avoid any experience of deception among customers[8].

Application of Emotional Scarcity in Strategies

Integrating emotional scarcity into your persuasion strategies can strength motion. Use terms like «restricted version,» «available for a restrained time,» or «particular» to create a enjoy of urgency. Highlight the ideal blessings individuals can gain through appearing rapid.

Example: Video streaming systems which includes Netflix leverage emotional scarcity via the use of an powerful advertising and marketing tactic to inspire subscribers to watch content material at once. When new content cloth cloth, whether or not a TV series or a documentary, is uploaded to Netflix, the platform may additionally pick to make it available for a restrained time. This desire creates an artificial belief of shortage at some stage in the content material fabric, as subscribers understand that in the occasion that they don't watch it speedy, it would now not be to be had at the platform. This encourages subscribers to take right away movement and watch the content material cloth fabric earlier than it's taken down. This time strain reinforces the urgency of the state of affairs and may reason extended viewership, as subscribers want to seize the possibility on the identical time because it lasts. The effectiveness of this tactic rests on the mental precept of the worry of lacking out. Humans have a tendency to feature higher fee to opportunities that appear constrained in time, as they don't need to experience excluded or leave out out on some thing precise. This creates an intrinsic motivation to behave hastily and seize the opportunity on the equal time because it's to be had.

In the context of streaming structures, emotional shortage can help generate more potent call for for unique content material cloth, boom subscriber engagement, and create buzz round the ones titles. However, it may moreover draw grievance if subscribers sense rushed or within the occasion that they understand the content fabric fabric to be artificially restricted to beautify viewership.

The Traps and Ethics of Emotional Scarcity

While emotional shortage is a powerful approach, it have to be used ethically.

Exaggerating shortage or developing faux limitations can reason distrust and loss of purchaser self guarantee. The purpose need to continuously be to create a actual feel of a completely particular opportunity.

Example: Imagine a employer launching a product and claiming that it's in very confined amount, therefore suggesting that clients want to buy it quick to now not pass over out on the opportunity. However, in reality, the business enterprise has enough stock of the product to fulfill the selection for. In this case, the organisation is leveraging the worry of missing out (FOMO) with the resource of the usage of the belief of scarcity to activate clients to make a quick purchase choice. But if clients find out that the product wasn't as scarce as they notion, it is able to have horrific effects on the company's recognition. Deceiving customers by way of manner of falsely claiming that a product is in confined quantity even as it's not can cause emotions of distrust and disappointment among customers. They also can sense manipulated and lose self belief within the corporation corporation. This deception can not simplest harm brief-term earnings however additionally have an prolonged-time period effect on the brand's relationship with its customers. Integrity and transparency are essential elements for keeping consumer accept as true with. When a organization uses emotional shortage in reality and ethically, it may beautify the attraction of its merchandise and encourage purchaser engagement. However, if this tactic is used deceptively, it could have terrible and disappointing repercussions on the business enterprise's perception and its dating with its clients.

Chapter 5: The Magnetic Authority

The Brilliance of Magnetic Authority

Magnetic authority is built at the concept that people are more inclined to study folks that very own information and deep records in a specific location. When you encompass authority with self belief, you radiate credibility and inspire take into account.

Example: Imagine a expert event along with a conference or seminar. The organizers have selected to invite a speaker, a extensively diagnosed expert of their field, to percent their understanding and revel in with the target audience. The presence of this speaker adds a length of credibility to the occasion.

The authority right here stems from the established reputation of the speaker as an expert in their area. Their records is stated with the aid of manner of peers and the target audience, lending them high credibility. Event attendees are interested by the possibility to look at at once from the form of knowledgeable supply.

As the speaker takes the stage, their speech is infused with deep records and advanced knowledge of the task. Their language, examples, and analyses display off their information, in addition improving the feel of authority they emanate.

By taking part in this event, attendees are uncovered to this magnetic authority. They revel in that the speaker's statistics is a precious supply of statistics and concept. They are encouraged to pay attention attentively, ask applicable questions, and take in the shared teachings.

The example illustrates how the presence of an established authority can upload massive cost to an event. It draws an audience inquisitive about the opportunity to have a look at from top resources and have interaction in intellectually stimulating exchanges.

The Fusion of Knowledge and Trust

Magnetic authority rests on a sensitive balance among expertise and acquire as real with. Possessing expertise is vital, but the functionality to speak empathetically and encourage agree with is in addition important in establishing substantial connections.

Example: Steve Jobs, the visionary founding father of Apple, perfectly embodies magnetic authority. His adventure is a masterful demonstration of the electricity of balancing understanding and keep in mind in building tremendous bonds.

Endowed with smooth technical know-how, Steve Jobs unique the tech organization thru his deep facts of progressive products and answers. However, what genuinely set Jobs apart come to be his capability to talk this expertise in a way that captivated and inspired others. His aura and vision compelled humans to really take delivery of as real with in his thoughts and accept as true with him, growing magnetic authority.

An iconic example is the release of the iPhone in 2007. Steve Jobs added this innovative tool with such conviction and ardour that the goal marketplace emerge as right away captivated. He controlled to offer an cause of the complex skills of the cellphone in an reachable manner at the equal time as evoking exhilaration and don't forget. His combination of technical expertise and empathetic verbal exchange created an air of mystery of magnetic authority, remodeling Apple right into a global cultural phenomenon.

Steve Jobs additionally showcased how the steadiness among understanding and trust can be critical in building relationships. His capacity to pay attention to consumer goals and offer merchandise that catered to their dreams bolstered purchaser accept as true with in the Apple logo. He long-established emotional connections with the aid of manner of sharing his very own values and telling powerful stories about how Apple products can also want to decorate humans's lives.

In give up, Steve Jobs perfectly illustrates how magnetic authority is constructed via using merging technical information with empathetic and galvanizing verbal exchange. His legacy endures as a management model that suggests the manner to installation tremendous bonds through combining records and take into account.

The Effect of Authority on Perceptions

Authority has a powerful impact on how humans recognize and respond to information. Individuals are extra willing to truely be given and have a look at the advice of an authoritative determine, assuming that this man or woman is aware about what's first rate for them.

Example: Let's recollect the case of Arianna Huffington, the founding father of HuffPost, a identified man or woman in the realm of virtual media and intellectual nicely-being.

Her have an effect on as an authoritative voice in this vicinity has a top notch effect on how people understand recommendation and information related to nicely-being. Take the example of a person named Alex, who's seeking out strategies to beautify their highbrow properly-being. By analyzing articles and searching motion photos from HuffPost, Alex is uncovered to thoughts and recommendation shared by means of manner of the use of Arianna Huffington. Arianna's credibility as an expert parent inside the place turns on Alex to pay precise hobby to her advice. When Alex comes in the path of an interview wherein Arianna openly discusses her very personal opinions of burnout and strategies she followed to decorate her highbrow health, it profoundly influences Alex's belief. She regards this recommendation as reliable and applicable because of the authority Arianna holds in the discipline. Over time, Alex places into exercise meditation strategies, art work-existence balance, and stress management strategies advocated with the aid of Arianna. She observes tangible improvements in her highbrow properly-being and begins offevolved sharing her revel in with others, encouraging them to furthermore follow Arianna's recommendation. This instance illustrates how Arianna Huffington's authority acts as a easy out that influences how Alex perceives and integrates intellectual well-being recommendation. The impact of Arianna's authority effects in prolonged self belief in this advice, showcasing how authority can play a key function in how human beings compare and adopt records from influential figures in a given challenge.

Embodying Magnetic Authority in Practice

Embodying magnetic authority requires ongoing acquisition of understanding and powerful communique of that knowledge. Share your knowledge via speeches, articles, blogs, or movies. Use concrete examples and anecdotes to illustrate your elements and make the facts more available.

Example: When delivering a professional presentation, setting up your authority and credibility from the outset is crucial. This can be achieved with the aid of the use of highlighting your revel in and records in the challenge you're addressing. By sharing your achievements, qualifications, and applicable ancient beyond, you showcase to your target market that you have legitimacy to speak at the issue. Once you've mounted credibility, it's vital to provide valuable and applicable facts. This showcases your deep understanding of the priority and reinforces your authority recognition. Offering information, data, concrete examples, and in-depth evaluation permits your audience to recognize that you have mastered the trouble and characteristic done critical studies. Clear and attractive conversation is likewise essential. Use expert language and keep away from excessive jargon that would alienate your target market. Structure your presentation logically, introducing ideas progressively and linking them coherently. You also can encompass relevant testimonies or anecdotes to demonstrate your elements and seize your target audience's interest. In precis, thru way of beginning with putting in your credibility as an professional and sooner or later handing over in-depth and attractive information, you enhance your authority for the duration of your expert presentation. This allows your goal market to view you as a reliable supply of statistics and mind, thereby bolstering the impact of your message.

Applying Magnetic Authority in Strategies

Integrating magnetic authority into your persuasion techniques calls for normal demonstration of your knowledge. Use testimonials from glad customers, expert certifications, and examples of success to strengthen your authority. Share your statistics through awesome academic content material.

Example: Online influencers who percent advice specifically domain names, such as health or vitamins, are a concrete example of the usage of magnetic authority to advantage the agree with and engagement in their intention market. In in recent times's digital global, many human beings trying to find advice and information online to decorate their fitness, nicely-being, and way of life. Influencers who've evolved apparent know-how especially regions can grow to be assets of concept and guidance for his or her fans. Their capability to share deep statistics, provide an reason for complicated thoughts in an on hand way, and provide practical advice distinguishes their content cloth from the abundance of records available online. By cultivating their private expertise and staying informed about the modern day studies of their field, those influencers set up credibility and authority with their goal market. Thoughtful use of real proof, collectively with references to medical research, personal testimonials, and achievements, bolsters their legitimacy as professionals. Their continued engagement with their target market—answering questions, presenting customized recommendation, and sharing their private research—contributes to constructing a relied

49

on reference to their fanatics. As a end result, those influencers can definitely have an impact at the options and behaviors in their target marketplace related to health, nutrients, and other associated domain names. This instance demonstrates how magnetic authority can be legitimately used to inspire and guide a web goal marketplace towards choices useful for his or her well-being and health.

The Ethics of Magnetic Authority

Magnetic authority need to be used with integrity. Representing expertise or expertise you don't own can erode receive as real with and tarnish your recognition. Be obvious about your revel in and maintain to broaden your abilties.

Example: Online «specialists» who declare records in areas they don't in reality apprehend are a concrete instance that highlights the dangers of unfounded magnetic authority. In the digital global, it has turn out to be common to look humans presenting themselves as experts, offering advice and information in severa⸱ fields together with nicely-being, rate range, fitness, and in addition. However, these self-proclaimed experts frequently lack actual and strong information in the regions they declare to grasp. Their loss of actual competence can rapid be exposed on the same time as their content fabric is significantly evaluated thru specialists or human beings with real revel in inside the field. Factual errors, wrong statistics, or unfounded recommendation can query their credibility and weaken their authority. This phenomenon underscores the importance of deliver verification and thorough research even as considering on line records. Informed audiences are an increasing number of skeptical and are seeking out tangible proof of someone's facts in advance than granting their bear in mind. The instance of online «experts» serves as a reminder that real magnetic authority is built on right facts and actual revel in in a selected difficulty, in desire to drain and unfounded claims.

Chapter 6: Reciprocal Engagement

The Magic of Reciprocal Engagement

Reciprocal engagement is constructed at the not unusual precept of reciprocity. When you supply something of price to a person, they are extra willing to offer something lower again to you. This method strengthens bonds and creates a experience of splendid indebtedness.

Example: When you pick out to distribute unfastened samples of your product, you capitalize at the precept of reciprocal engagement. By offering a few issue of price without the obligation to make a purchase, you create a dynamic wherein clients feel indebted in your enterprise. This symbolic debt of appreciation motivates them to seriously do not forget shopping for the entire product. Reciprocal engagement works through manner of exploiting the human desire to healthy first-rate moves with same excessive nice actions. When you provide a free sample, you establish an initial dating based totally on selfless giving. In circulate returned, customers revel in a duty to reciprocate by way of way of manner of selecting to shop for the whole product. This psychological phenomenon underlies many free trial and sampling applications within the enterprise global. By encouraging a risk-unfastened initial determination, you pave the way for a deeper and collectively useful commercial business enterprise relationship.

Building Connections through Reciprocal Engagement

Reciprocal engagement creates a dynamic of cooperation and take into account. Individuals are obviously influenced to go back the want and contribute definitely. This method may be used to reinforce personal and professional relationships.

Example: When you pick out to offer useful and applicable recommendation to a colleague or buddy, you installation a bond of reciprocity. This bond primarily based totally on the concept that during case you've taken the time to function price to a person's life, they'll be willing to reciprocate while you need help inside the destiny. This dynamic is rooted in the principle of reciprocal engagement, wherein the act of giving creates a feel of ethical duty to reply in a comparable way. By imparting useful advice, you display goodwill and an intention to assist. This movement creates a perceived social debt, wherein the man or woman you've helped feels a form of ethical duty to do you a choice in move returned. This can appear in various methods, whether it's providing direct useful resource, sharing resources, or clearly being more willing to pay attention and help while you're in want. This example illustrates how reciprocal engagement works in ordinary interactions. By giving first, you establish a basis of trust and goodwill, making it more likely that others will respond clearly at the same time as you're in want. This technique can be strategically employed to bolster relationships and domesticate enduring, jointly beneficial bonds.

The Effect of Consistency and Positive Debt

Reciprocal engagement is based totally mostly on the human need for consistency and honoring commitments. Once someone commits to a few trouble small, they're much more likely to dedicate similarly to live constant with their initial behavior. This creates a cycle of terrific debt.

Example: When a person subscribes to a brand's e-e-e-newsletter or mailing list, they're making an act of initial engagement. This act may additionally seem minor, but it creates a form of determination to the emblem. This dynamic is primarily based on the idea of cognitive consistency, suggesting that human beings will be inclined to act in line with their preceding commitments and choices. Once a person has made the choice to enroll in a e-book, they've expressed initial interest within the statistics, products, or services the brand offers. This motion creates a enjoy of belonging or affiliation with the brand. Subsequently, while the brand sends information, product tips, or unique gives thru its publication, the character is greater willing to react really. This incredible response is driven through the usage of the herbal preference to be regular with past picks. Individuals commonly select to keep away from contradictions and act in line with their earlier commitments. Thus, a person who committed to subscribing to a e-e-publication is much more likely to view the products or tips from the equal emblem favorably, as it aligns with their preliminary choice. This example demonstrates how initial commitment can have an effect on subsequent attitudes and behaviors. It additionally illustrates how manufacturers can leverage this dynamic via building more potent relationships with their target market, capitalizing on preceding engagement, and supplying relevant records and charge via their communications.

Cultivating Reciprocal Engagement

Cultivating reciprocal engagement entails imparting price earlier than asking for anything in pass back. This can take the shape of recommendation, loose property, facts sharing, or selfless help. The cause is to bring together a agree with-based totally truely dating.

Example: Companies that offer free webinars offer their aim marketplace an opportunity to access exquisite facts and sensible advice in an interactive on-line layout. By doing so, they invent a space in which reciprocal engagement can flourish. When a organisation hosts a webinar, it demonstrates an investment in sharing expertise and the expert improvement of its audience. Webinar humans understand this providing as a threat to research, cope with precise troubles, or acquire new skills. In change for his or her time and participation, they get hold of price inside the form of applicable and useful facts. This alternate creates a sense of reciprocity. Participants understand the agency as having invested of their boom and development. In go back, they are more willing to understand this price via manner of manner of thinking about destiny interactions with the enterprise business enterprise—whether or not or now not or no longer it's purchasing products or services, signing up for other paid webinars, or recommending the enterprise to others. The feeling of reciprocal engagement is reinforced by the usage of the truth that the agency gave some thing of fee in advance than asking for something in go back. Participants experience a shape of obligation, that can create a stronger emotional bond amongst them and the agency. Ultimately, this example suggests how companies can cultivate high high-quality and lasting relationships with their target marketplace thru imparting reading possibilities and rate via free webinars. By setting up this form of reciprocal engagement, businesses can lay a strong foundation for fruitful future interactions with their goal marketplace.

Applying Reciprocal Engagement in Strategies

Incorporating reciprocal engagement into your persuasion techniques technique offering price first without searching ahead to immediately returns. Create valuable content fabric cloth, provide loose sources, and without a doubt manual others. Build sturdy relationships that actually support.

Example: The example illustrates how manufacturers can decorate reciprocal engagement through offering free, treasured content material fabric material to their clients. This approach is based on the precept that when organizations provide beneficial and relevant resources to their target audience, they set up a bond of reciprocity. Customers, having benefited from this introduced fee, are more willing to aid those brands in flow once more. Consider a fitness commercial organisation enterprise employer that offers a free guide on excellent practices for wholesome ingesting and an lively lifestyle. By providing this guide, the industrial company organisation offers precious, tangible records to its target market, helping them gain their well-being dreams. Consumers who use this guide can enjoy tangible consequences and feel grateful to the emblem for this remarkable contribution to their lives. Reciprocal engagement develops as producers assemble a depended on courting with their goal market thru concrete, beneficial moves. Customers apprehend the emblem as a dependable deliver of know-how and property, making them much more likely to guide it in the destiny. This example also demonstrates how the charge furnished in advance could have an impact on next shopping choices. When human beings apprehend the first rate and usability of the supplied unfastened content, they're more likely to discover the paid products or services provided with the aid of the emblem. This transition from loose price to paid rate is supported by the usage of way of the do not forget mounted through reciprocal engagement. In summary, this situation illustrates how brands can enhance their reciprocal engagement with their target audience via imparting useful and free resources. By presenting value upfront, organizations installation a endure in mind-primarily based totally courting which can in truth impact clients' destiny buying choices.

The Ethics and Integrity of Reciprocal Engagement

Reciprocal engagement want to be real and without hidden expectations. Giving with the motive of receiving immediately or manipulating others might be perceived as inauthentic and harm your prolonged-time period relationships. Integrity and sincerity are essential.

Example: The example illustrates a scenario wherein a person offers their assist selflessly however with hidden expectancies of receiving some factor in cross back. This behavior can often motive misunderstandings and feelings of manipulation, as undisclosed expectancies create an imbalance inside the relationship a number of the person offering assist and the only receiving it. Imagine a chum spontaneously offers to help you with a undertaking you're walking on. Initially, you is probably grateful and apprehend the generosity in their offer. However, if later you understand that this friend clearly anticipated some thing in go returned, which includes a similar want within the future or precise favors, it may regulate your belief of the initial help. Unexpressed expectancies can create a feel of deceit or manipulation. The individual who provided selfless help may in all likelihood have appeared altruistic, however in reality, that that they had hidden reasons. This can depart the possibility character feeling used or manipulated because of the reality they weren't informed of the conditions linked to the supplied help. In this context, transparency and open communication are important for keeping wholesome relationships.

Chapter 7: The Significance of Consistency

The Power of Consistency

Consistency is primarily based on the principle that people choose out to behave constant with their beliefs, values, and previous commitments. When your behavior aligns collectively with your beyond guarantees, others perceive your credibility and reliability.

Example: Imagine a business enterprise that highlights its determination to environmental sustainability in its public communications. It may additionally moreover use slogans, advertisements, and marketing and advertising and marketing campaigns to emphasize its problem for lowering its environmental effect (GreenTech innovators, Healthy food Chains, Fashion Ethique Brand). However, if this corporation fails to take concrete steps to put in force sustainable and environmentally high-quality practices, it risks compromising its reputation and credibility. The phenomenon right here is in the context of public don't forget and emblem photograph. When a employer proclaims a willpower to a noble purpose like environmental sustainability, it creates expectancies among stakeholders, along with clients, traders, and society at large. People expect consistency between the company's terms and actions. Furthermore, the impact is going past the patron dating. Investors and commercial agency partners furthermore price a organization's credibility and integrity. Inconsistency between stated values and actual movements can purpose economic and jail effects. In precis, the example suggests how a agency that publicizes a determination to environmental sustainability is anticipated to aid those words with concrete moves. Failing to accomplish that can have horrible repercussions on its popularity, credibility, and stakeholder relationships. This underscores the importance of alignment among communication and movements in maintaining a first-rate emblem picture and lasting agree with.

The Effect of Public Commitment and Personal Norm

Consistency is rooted inside the concept of personal norms. Once a person publicly commits to a few issue, they may be more likely to act according with that willpower to preserve their very personal fantastic photograph. This is based totally mostly on the selection to be regular with what we're announcing and do.

Example: Cialdini and his colleagues achieved a look at that highlights the super impact of public dedication on individuals' conduct, specially as regards to balloting in political elections. In this take a look at, individuals had been divided into groups. The first business enterprise changed into in reality asked about their purpose to vote in the approaching elections, without any form of determination. The 2nd group, instead, have come to be invited to make a public commitment thru signing a assertion indicating their intention to vote. This statement have grow to be displayed prominently for special members to appearance. The results placed out a considerable distinction among the 2 corporations. Participants within the 2d company, people who had made a public determination, were more likely to truely vote within the elections than the ones in the first institution. This finding highlights the energy of public determination in influencing humans' behavior. Public dedication acts as a mechanism of consistency. When someone makes a public determination, they revel in greater obligated to honor that willpower that allows you to be consistent with the picture they projected to others. In the context of the instance, individuals who signed the overall public statement felt more responsible and willing to vote, as their determination changed into now identified and seen to others. This illustrates how public self-control can play a important characteristic in reinforcing desired behaviors. By publicly pointing out their reason, individuals enjoy a experience of responsibility to themselves and others. This dynamic similarly motivates people to act in keeping with their determination, that would have a superb effect on behaviors which encompass voting, adopting sustainable adjustments, or every different particular purpose. In cease, the instance highlights how people are much more likely to conform with via whilst their commitment is made public. This underscores the powerful impact of public dedication on conduct, emphasizing people' tendency to act continuously with their public statements.

Encouraging Action Through Consistency

Encouraging motion via consistency involves reminding of beyond commitments and aligning messages with those commitments. Use reminders of preceding ensures to encourage others to behave in concord with their earlier commitments.

Example: In the context of fundraising campaigns, consistency is a powerful mental lever used to inspire donors to uphold their determination to a specific reason. This approach is primarily based at the concept that humans select to act continuously with their past commitments and movements. When someone makes a preference to donate to a certain cause, they make a self-control to that purpose. However, as quickly because the donation is made and the preliminary second of commitment has exceeded, specific priorities or distractions can also furthermore take over. This is in which consistency comes into play. Fundraising campaigns frequently rent strategies to remind donors of their preliminary commitment to the motive. This can be finished thru emails, social media posts, physical letters, or exceptional sorts of communication. For instance, a charitable enterprise might in all likelihood deliver an e-mail to a donor bringing up their previous donation and highlighting the high excellent effect it had. The reminder of this dedication creates a experience of consistency within the donor. Individuals regularly need to be in keeping with their past movements and values. Thus, while the donor is reminded of their initial dedication to the cause, they will be greater inclined to hold supporting that purpose because it reinforces their non-public consistency. In specific phrases, the donor is more stimulated to hold their manual to remain in harmony with their preceding selection to make a donation. The feeling of consistency performs an essential feature in influencing the donor's future behavior. This instance illustrates how consistency may be strategically used in the realm of fundraising to hold donor engagement. By reminding donors of their preliminary commitment and growing a consistency dynamic, fundraising campaigns can inspire donors to uphold their monetary help and keep contributing to the cause they care about.

Applying Consistency in Strategies

Integrating consistency into your persuasion techniques means first honoring your beyond commitments and aligning your moves collectively with your terms. Use reminders of preceding commitments to encourage motion. Create an surroundings wherein determination to your dreams is supported.

Example: Imagine that you've decided to art work for your health and health. You've devoted to regular workout exercises and a balanced diet regime. Initially, you're brought about and passionate about wearing out your goals. However, over the years, you discover it increasingly hard to maintain this willpower. Daily existence distractions, art work strain, and amazing duties start taking up. This is at the same time as you recognize the significance of integrating consistency into your efforts. You determine to apply a way of reminding your self of beyond commitments. You have a look at in your calendar the times and times you initially planned to education consultation. Every time you check some time desk, the ones notifications remind you of your initial dedication to your health. Furthermore, you create an surroundings supportive of your dreams. You put together your kitchen to have healthful food without a trouble available, therefore eliminating awful meals temptations. You choose out to enroll in a exercise group or find out a exercising associate, motivating you to stay everyday. As you maintain this consistency amongst your terms and actions, you begin noticing development for your health and health. Your exercising intervals turn out to be a dependancy, and you experience extra active and assured. By integrating consistency into your non-public persuasion strategies, you've converted your initial commitment into ongoing, massive motion.

Ethics and Transparency of Consistency

Consistency ought to be used ethically and transparently. Not following through on beyond commitments or manipulating others into performing opposite to their values can be distressing for the individual and lead to lack of undergo in mind and a tarnished popularity.

Chapter 8: The Magic of Persuasive Storytelling

The Story of Persuasive Storytelling

Persuasive storytelling is built at the capability of memories to evoke emotions and create a personal connection. By telling a story, you create an emotional context that makes information greater memorable and convincing.

Example: When a nicely being agency stocks the inspiring story of a consumer who converted their health via their merchandise, they rent a approach of persuasive storytelling to set up an emotional bond with capability customers. This method goes beyond easy product merchandising and dreams to create an right connection through highlighting the real great impact the products had on someone's lifestyles. In this case, the fitness corporation harnesses the electricity of testimonials to beautify their credibility and authority. By sharing an genuine fulfillment story, they display that their merchandise aren't just merchandise, however tangible solutions that can enhance human beings' lives. This technique is robust as it movements a chord with capability customers who are searching for concrete proof of product effectiveness. The transformation story of the consumer creates an emotional connection via eliciting empathy and identification from capacity clients who may additionally relate to similar situations. This allows capacity customers to visualise the outstanding consequences they could accumulate with the aid of the use of the usage of the use of the business enterprise's merchandise. Such visualization can be a powerful trouble in influencing their purchase alternatives. By sharing success memories, the corporation moreover employs the technique of social evidence, as noted in Chapter 3, demonstrating that others have already benefited from their merchandise. This can bolster capability clients' self belief within the fantastic and effectiveness of the goods, thereby encouraging them to strive the products themselves. In precis, achievement memories create an emotional connection and provide social evidence. This persuasive technique can effect capability clients thru displaying that products have a actual and tangible impact on human beings's lives, improving attention and interest in the organization's merchandise.

Creating an Emotional Connection

Persuasive storytelling establishes an emotional connection some of the speaker and the target market. Emotions shared in a story may have an effect on listeners' attitudes and behaviors, making them extra receptive to messages and thoughts.

Example: Imagine a speaker at a TEDx occasion. They share their private revel in of overcoming a large failure to demonstrate the power of persuasive storytelling. They begin via way of recounting how they launched a promising startup, invested severa hours and belongings, simplest to stand a powerful failure that precipitated the commercial enterprise organisation's closure. They evoke the extreme feelings they felt—discouragement, frustration, and lack of shallowness. They describe the immediate they needed to announce to their organization and buyers that their venture come to be unexpectedly ending. The shared emotions in the narrative create an empathetic connection with the goal marketplace, allowing them to sense the ache of failure and its emotional impact. However, they don't prevent there. They offer an motive of ways they selected to show this failure proper proper into a reading and boom opportunity. They describe the stairs they took to get higher, reflect on education located out, and reinvent themselves. Through persuasive storytelling, they not most effective percent feelings but moreover the journey they embarked on to conquer limitations. By connecting their personal story to broader necessities, they exhibit how feelings shared in a story should have an impact on attitudes and behaviors. They emphasize how authenticity and vulnerability in storytelling can installation a deep connection with the target audience, making them more receptive to messages of reading and perception.

The Effect of Memorability and Persuasion

Persuasive storytelling represents an effective approach for boosting statistics retention in communication. Incorporating emotional and narrative factors into speech will boom memorability, maximum essential to better understanding and retention of messages. These elements permit listeners to emotionally engage with the content material, strengthening their attachment to the provided statistics. Consequently, records turns into extra available in lengthy-time period memory, that could in the long run have an effect on listeners' choices and alternatives associated with the subjects stated.

Example: Imagine a passionate shop clerk running at a Porsche dealership, devoted to showcasing the logo's current-day iconic sports activities car. When a capability client walks into the showroom, the shop clerk warmly welcomes them and invitations them to take a seat down down for a communicate. Instead of genuinely list technical functions, the store clerk involves a selection to use persuasive storytelling to captivate their purchaser's hobby. They start thru sharing Porsche's wealthy and prestigious data, recounting the organisation's humble beginnings and mythical successes on race circuits throughout the arena. The shop clerk underscores how each Porsche model embodies this way of life of modern-day-day engineering and powerful feelings. They then delve into the statistics of the car before them. Instead of focusing solely on overall performance numbers, they narrate the tale of the meticulous format of every issue. They percentage how engineers aimed to capture the essence of herbal sporty the use of on the identical time as integrating advanced era for an notable driving revel in. The salesperson uses anecdotes from song checks and remarks from exclusive delighted customers to illustrate the emotional impact of the use of a

Porsche. They inspire the customer to check the sensations of pace, control, and beauty they may experience at the back of the wheel. By integrating emotional factors into their presentation, the salesperson creates a profound connection some of the client and the automobile. The narrative facts make the acquisition of a Porsche an emotionally charged and significant experience. Later, while the consumer shows on their choice, the top notch feelings evoked with the resource of the store clerk's persuasive storytelling will play a key feature of their choice to collect this top notch sports sports activities car. Thus, persuasive storytelling enhances expertise, statistics retention, and have an effect on over selections, contributing to shaping significant and lasting trying to find stories for Porsche clients.

Application of Persuasive Storytelling in Strategies

Integrating persuasive storytelling into your persuasion techniques first entails figuring out the emotional and narrative elements that help your key messages. Tell stories that encompass your values and desires, thereby developing an emotional connection with your target market.

Example: Imagine a organization that crafts artisanal products the usage of conventional techniques. Instead of completely that specialize in product capabilities, the organization chooses to percent the story inside the once more of the muse of its products. They give an cause of how these artisanal strategies had been surpassed down through generations, highlighting the dedication and statistics of those who practiced them. By telling this story, the commercial enterprise agency forges an emotional bond with its clients. Buyers start to see the products as greater than mere commodities; they view them due to the fact the end stop end result of a cultural statistics and cherished traditions. This emotional connection offers more fee to the products, as clients are now invested inside the story on the returned of each object they purchase. Furthermore, producers that percent the reminiscences of the people at the back of their corporation allow customers to get to recognize the faces and values using the commercial enterprise employer. This can create a experience of closeness and undergo in mind, as customers experience associated with the group behind the brand. Similarly, thru showcasing the splendid versions the emblem has added to humans or groups, the organisation demonstrates the way it genuinely contributes to society. The use of such testimonies has a massive effect. On one hand, they help differentiate the brand within the market with the useful resource of manner of making a completely unique and emotional narrative. On the alternative hand, they decorate consumer engagement with the emblem, as there may be now a private tale related to the products or services they purchase. Ultimately, those narratives assist purchaser loyalty to the logo and make a contribution to building an prolonged-term relationship. In summary, this example illustrates how manufacturers that percent tales approximately the muse in their products, the humans inside the lower back in their corporation, or the super differences they've introduced approximately can create effective emotional bonds with customers, differentiate their brand, and beautify patron engagement.

Ethics and Authenticity of Persuasive Storytelling

Persuasive storytelling must be actual and ethical. Fabricated or exaggerated memories may be perceived as manipulative and harm believe. Narratives ought to be based on reality and resonate with real feelings.

Example: Imagine a business organization identifying to percent its adventure thru an genuine tale. Instead of definitely selling its products or services, it chooses to relate the demanding situations it confronted and the steps taken to triumph over them. By sharing the highs and lows of its adventure, the business enterprise humanizes its brand and establishes a deeper reference to its purpose marketplace. By exposing the difficult moments it encountered, the organization shows vulnerability and transparency. This openness creates a revel in of believe, due to the reality the audience perceives the enterprise enterprise as right and honest. Additionally, through using sharing classes located out at every degree, the industrial employer enterprise gives delivered rate to its goal market with the aid of sharing sensible insights and treasured teachings. The effect of this narrative method is multifaceted. Firstly, it captures the goal marketplace's interest, as actual testimonies are often more engaging than traditional advertising and marketing messages. Secondly, it conjures up emotion, because the stressful situations conquer and successes achieved are inherently human elements that resonate with humans' evaluations. Lastly, it strengthens loyalty to the emblem, because the audience feels associated and may pick out with the shared challenges and triumphs. In essence, this situation suggests how the use of an right tale can create a profound and lasting connection amongst a organization and its goal market thru setting up a basis of take delivery of as proper with, generating emotion, and imparting real charge.

BONUS: THE REVOLUTION OF AI-ASSISTED NEGOTIATION

From one display show display to some other, the digital technology opens new views in the artwork of persuasion. In this bonus financial ruin, we're capable of explore the modern tendencies of effect, fueled through synthetic intelligence (AI), augmented truth (AR), and distinct growing technology. By seizing these possibilities, you will become a pioneer of have an impact on in the ever-evolving international.

The Impact of AI on Persuasion

Artificial intelligence is revolutionizing how we have interaction and have an effect on. AI systems examine behavioral records to personalize pointers and messages, that can decorate the effectiveness of persuasion.

Example: Social media systems like Facebook, Instagram, and Twitter integrate modern day synthetic intelligence (AI) algorithms to customise the content material fabric exhibited to each patron. These algorithms go through in thoughts a multitude of facts, which incorporates beyond interactions, declared hobbies, browsing conduct, and demographic facts. The goal is to create a more appealing character revel in with the aid of offering content material cloth cloth that is supposed to be applicable and interesting to every individual. The effect of this personalization goes beyond in reality displaying unique posts or advertisements. Based on what the character sees, likes, shares, and comments on, algorithms continuously regulate content material material material recommendations to align with their presumed opportunities and reviews. This creates an records bubble wherein users are especially uncovered to viewpoints similar to their very very own, as a result reinforcing their present day beliefs and evaluations. This phenomenon might also have a big effect on how customers recognize the sector, form critiques, and make selections. AI algorithms no longer at once have an effect on person picks by means of presenting records that aligns with their pre-present beliefs. This could make stronger cognitive biases and create polarization of critiques, as customers are much less exposed to specific perspectives. In the example of social media structures, using AI to customize content cloth illustrates how persuasive techniques may be executed on a massive scale to influence consumer opportunities and evaluations. It also highlights the importance of being privy to this ability manipulation and actively searching for pretty a few facts property to advantage a balanced attitude. The same applies to tune streaming structures.

The Augmented Reality Experience

Augmented fact opens up new possibilities for influencing perceptions. By masking virtual elements onto the actual global, producers can create immersive evaluations which have an impact on attitudes and behaviors.

Example: The use of augmented truth by way of a furniture company represents a big improvement in how clients should make buying picks. This technology permits clients to in reality visualize furnishings of their very personal region, collectively with their residing room or bed room, earlier than searching for. This immersive visualization gives a very unique enjoy that could extensively have an effect on looking for decisions. When a consumer visits the furniture enterprise's net web site, they will be able to use the augmented fact function to overlay digital images of the preferred fixtures in their very very very own environment. This offers the consumer a completely specific concept of the way the furniture will look of their home and the way it's going to match with the rest of the room.

This visual revel in allows address one of the vital uncertainties of on-line purchasing: what will the product seem like in reality?

The impact of augmented fact goes past easy visualization. By allowing clients to appearance furniture of their very own area, the furniture employer creates a deeper revel in of engagement and reference to the goods. Customers can boom a more potent emotional attachment to the furniture they visualize of their very personal environment, that would beautify their choice to buy. Furthermore, this era reduces the perceived danger for clients at the same time as making online purchases. They have the opportunity to make greater informed selections as they may be able to determine the furniture's suit in their area even before ordering it. This can make a contribution to increasing customers' self guarantee of their choice, that would translate into better conversion costs and sales. In this example, the use of augmented reality to influence purchaser purchasing selections illustrates how an immersive and interactive revel in may additionally have a large effect on engagement, self warranty, and desire to shop for products.

Ethics and Transparency in Technology

The use of AI and unique generation for have an impact on will growth ethical questions. Brands want to be obvious about records series and usage. Users must additionally be aware of the functionality have an impact on of these technology.

Example: Data privateness scandals visit conditions in which businesses or companies were concerned in unauthorized series, use, or sharing of users' private information. These incidents have highlighted the crucial need for transparency and duty inside the use of influencing era, mainly in the virtual context. When a organization collects non-public data from its clients, whether thru internet sites, mobile apps, or other systems, it acquires a tremendous amount of touchy statistics. This can encompass records collectively with buy opportunities, surfing conduct, region records, or maybe in my opinion identifiable statistics. Using this information to steer customer conduct, which includes focused on precise advertisements, might also additionally have a tremendous effect on their choices. This has underscored the vital want for transparency, in which groups have to definitely monitor how they accumulate, use, and percent person records. Users need to be knowledgeable of ways their data may be used for customization and have an effect on functions. Regulations which embody the European Union's General Data Protection Regulation (GDPR) were put in vicinity to guard person rights and make certain that their personal statistics is processed ethically and transparently. Ultimately, data privateness scandals spotlight the critical importance of ethics and responsibility within the use of influencing era. Companies want to stability their intention of persuasion and personalization with respecting customers' privateness. Transparency, disclosure, and statistics safety are critical elements in building do not forget and avoiding privacy breaches that would tarnish businesses' reputations and disrupt the depended on courting with customers.

Striking the Balance Between Technology and Humanity

While developing generation provide new possibilities for have an effect on, the human detail stays vital. Authentic interactions, empathy, and expertise live crucial elements for constructing lasting relationships.

Example: Artificial intelligence (AI) chatbots have become increasingly commonplace in on-line customer support and assist structures. They are designed to offer short and automated responses to common questions and to assist users remedy easy issues. However, there are situations in which actual human interactions are critical to address more complicated problems and offer a deeper degree of assist.

Chatbots are effective in addressing easy and standardized queries. For example, they could offer facts about schedules, go back hints, or product capabilities. They are also beneficial for steering clients to the proper useful resource or branch based mostly on their request.

However, as issues grow to be extra complicated, consisting of troubleshooting technical problems, specific requests, or conditions that require contextual knowledge, chatbots may also moreover moreover show their barriers. Authentic human interactions are vital in the ones times for severa reasons:

Contextual Understanding: Complex troubles regularly require an intensive assessment of the context and history of the state of affairs. Humans can draw near the ones nuances and ask observe-up questions to benefit a greater correct information.

Empathy and Compassion: Issues concerning human emotions, troubles, or frustrations can advantage from human interplay. Human sellers can specific empathy and provide emotional beneficial resource, that is difficult to replicate with chatbots.

Creative Solutions: Complex troubles frequently require progressive and custom designed answers. Humans can advise precise techniques based totally genuinely on the scenario, at the same time as chatbots observe pre-programmed scripts.

Adaptation to Interaction: Human interactions are bendy and adaptive. If a user doesn't understand a response or goals further explanation, human dealers can adapt and rephrase facts in notable techniques. This is the inspiration of powerful communication.

In precis, AI chatbots are treasured system for offering quick and automatic responses in smooth scenarios. However, even as complicated problems require deep expertise, empathy, and innovative solutions, actual human interactions are important to offer a exquisite stage of assist and comprehensively remedy issues. The aggregate of AI and human outlets can for this reason be an powerful approach to provide entire and remarkable customer service.

The Prudent Application of Technology

Use growing technology carefully and in alignment with ethical values. Understand the blessings and limitations of these system and ensure they decorate persuasion with out compromising integrity.

Example: The use of synthetic intelligence (AI) to personalize gives has emerge as a common workout for lots businesses, especially in e-alternate, on line marketing and advertising, and advertising and marketing and advertising and advertising. The cause of this personalization is to offer customers with merchandise, services, or suggestions that suit their alternatives and person goals. However, for this approach to be effective, it's crucial that the pointers generated by using the usage of the use of AI are relevant and aligned with customers' actual needs. Here are some key elements to don't forget:

Accurate Data Collection: To personalize gives in a applicable way, corporations have to accumulate correct data on customer opportunities, searching for conduct, and behaviors. This can include information collectively with purchase histories, visited pages, clicks, and interactions at the net internet web page.

Analysis and Machine Learning: The amassed information is then processed by way of way of device analyzing algorithms that become aware of styles and dispositions. The higher AI can apprehend clients' beyond behaviors and possibilities, the more correct future tips can be.

Customer Segmentation: Customers need to be segmented into comparable agencies based mostly on commonplace tendencies and behaviors. This allows AI to customise guidelines based totally on every group's particular capabilities.

Evaluation of Recommendations: AI-generated tips want to be evaluated for their relevance to each consumer. If a recommendation doesn't in form the customer's goals or appears inappropriate, it is able to bring about dissatisfaction and lack of take delivery of as genuine with.

Feedback and Adjustments: Companies need to gather patron feedback on customized guidelines. Positive or terrible comments can assist refine algorithms and enhance the relevance of destiny recommendations.

Privacy and Ethical Considerations: The use of data for personalisation want to be obvious and have a look at information protection regulations. Customers should have the functionality to manipulate the information they percentage and particular their alternatives regarding personalization.

In precis, the usage of AI to personalize gives can offer huge blessings via enhancing the customer revel in and riding income. However, for fulfillment, corporations must make sure that generated suggestions are relevant, aligned with customers' actual goals, and cling to privacy and moral requirements. AI-primarily based personalization need to motive to enhance perceived consumer charge at the equal time as retaining a apparent and privacy-respecting approach.

Chapter 9: Why Is This So Important?

An impact is, to area it actually, a person who, similarly to developing an entire lot of coins from their website or on line employer, can generate a number of buzz and, if critical, have an impact on public opinion. An "idea chief" is a person who can convince, inspire, and encourage others to once more a purpose.

A have an effect on is a logo-new class of movie megastar. Someone who has large popularity and can take advantage of the numerous exciting rewards that includes it.

Being an influencer moreover requires widely wide-spread economic safety and resilience. It implies that you aren't reliant on a unmarried item or carrier—you're the best or carrier! Businesses will pay you hundreds of bucks only to post a subsidized piece, which can also moreover furthermore incorporate now not something more complex than carrying their goods.

Additionally, you could supply them for your objects. Think approximately the opportunity of having an intention market of tens of lots, even hundreds of hundreds, of potential clients for each products or services that you offer! If the idea of getting even the slightest quantity of affect pursuits you, likely you need to undergo in thoughts turning into one.

Becoming an influencer also can cause collaborations with one of a kind producers and opportunities for subsidized content fabric that could generate additional profits and publicity on your non-public brand. It requires determination and hard artwork, however the capability rewards can be massive.

Additionally, one of the responsibilities that include having have an effect on is the responsibility to make exceptional use of the platform that you have. Many effective humans use their impact to help vital social motives, deliver interest to urgent troubles, and even exchange public insurance. When you have got the functionality to persuade others, you moreover may also have the functionality to virtually affect the sector round you. Developing a non-public brand inside the role of an influencer requires an method that is strategic. This way locating your market region of hobby, arising along side your non-public voice and style, and making content fabric this is every ordinary and of high nice. Achieving success furthermore calls that allows you to actively engage together along with your target demographic and cultivate relationships with other influential people in your difficulty. It is important to hold in mind that being an influencer is not always glamorous. This is some thing that need to be stored in thoughts. It requires regular attempt and backbone, similarly to the highbrow fortitude to cope with the negativity and complaint that can be found on the internet. In order to maintain one's intellectual and emotional fitness in specific popularity, it is crucial to have a stable community of human beings to lean on and to make looking after oneself a pinnacle priority. To summarize, turning into an influencer may be a profitable and profitable profession direction; however, at the way to achieve this place, you may want to put in a whole lot of tough paintings, be proper, and characteristic a right passion for your specific place. You can domesticate a successful personal logo and make a excessive fine impact on the arena via your affect in case you commit yourself fully and stay steadfast to your efforts

What Makes You a Powerful Influencer?

But the most critical query, "What exactly is an influencer?" has no clear reaction at this element. An influencer is someone who has access to a massive target market and might convince humans in that focus on goal marketplace to trade their minds or come to be inquisitive about a products or services.

To emerge as a effective influencer, one need to have a strong non-public emblem, be proper and obvious of their content fabric fabric, and interact with their audience often.

Additionally, having records in a particular area of interest and taking element with one-of-a-kind influencers also can boom one's impact.

A individual who has an entire lot of fanatics on YouTube or who's a well-known famous person on Instagram and has tens of plenty or maybe hundreds of masses of followers is a great instance of an influencer. Another possibility is the proprietor of a weblog whose articles are examine through a massive wide sort of human beings.

If you've got been to put up an eBook proper this 2d, do you accept as true with you studied human beings might be rushing to shop for it? Would posting a photograph of yourself on social media at the same time as carrying a selected object encourage others to ask about it and probably make a buy? If you responded "positive" to any of these questions, then you will be taken into consideration an influencer.

Is It Required to Be a Celebrity?

Is having a superstar reputation important to have influencer reputation?

First of all, it's miles no longer now not feasible to get a massive, dependable fan base with out already being well-known. Even if you achieve success, becoming a huge influencer might now not continually encompass amassing 1 million subscribers (even though it'd be incredible and a super motive to have).

The idea of a "micro-influencer" is some different. While they've got a significantly smaller intention marketplace, they are but influential and persuasive, making them a suitable goal for a prospective advertising and advertising organization.

Even if you simplest have five,000 Instagram enthusiasts however they're active, you may no matter the reality that create buzz. Moreover, if you have the right form of impact, this may have a domino impact and feature an effect on different critical influencers.

Some advertising groups discover that having a smaller influencer consisting of you is excellent thinking about that they recognize you'll charge much less even as despite the fact that having a huge effect on elevating brand popularity and the appeal in their product.

When it includes boosting income to your private agency, even a modest little little little bit of have an effect on may be pretty useful.

How to Build Your Strategy

Now that you understand what it takes to be an influencer, you is probably thinking how you could get there your self. What are some strategies you may make a name for yourself on-line as a effective influencer? The number one technique involved generating outstanding content material fabric material further to a "undertaking assertion" that is open and honest and then promoting that statistics on the net. Creating a "personal logo" is frequently an crucial a part of this machine. In exceptional terms, you may now not be using a logo or a business enterprise name due to the fact you will create your personal brand as an alternative.Four

Creating a Personal Brand

The concept of personal branding is each quite interesting and probably to seize the hobby of a amazing amount of people.

Personal branding basically entails turning your name and picture into your brand.

This gives clients the risk to possibly turn out to be on line minor celebrities (for that reason the big appeal!) and offers businesses the chance to speak with a much huge target audience in a extra significant and effective way.

Also, private branding enables you end up greater reachable and "human" with the aid of the use of the use of supporting you construct a greater direct reference to your goal marketplace. Because of this, you could have a higher danger of making actual pals and fanatics in vicinity of just customers or customers. Every company may additionally moreover significantly gain from a connection of this kind.

To create a private brand, it's far vital first of all the resource of identifying your specific strengths, talents, and values. Consider what devices you other than others in your organization and what message you need to deliver for your audience. Next, increase a steady visible identification, which includes a emblem and coloration scheme, that displays your private emblem. This will help set up reputation and make your emblem extra memorable. Consistency is important in building a non-public brand. This approach developing a cohesive message across all structures and keeping a ordinary tone of voice in your content material material. Engaging together along with your goal market is likewise vital in constructing a private brand. Respond to remarks and messages, and actively are seeking out out possibilities to collaborate with distinctive influencers on your corporation. It's essential to undergo in mind that private branding isn't approximately developing a fake personality or photo. It want to be a proper reflection of who you're and what you stand for. Building a personal emblem takes time and effort, however the blessings can be tremendous. It will let you stand out in a crowded market, installation credibility and accept as true with together together with your goal marketplace, and open up new opportunities for boom and success.

What makes it work?

There are numerous reasons why non-public branding is powerful, specially even as mixed with social media.

A personal logo, first and maximum important, offers your internet site and company a far extra intimate vibe, as though humans comprehend you and may connect to you. As a impact, people have a tendency to buy from you because of the truth they'll agree with they will be able to don't forget you.

The purpose right here is to emerge as a person who exclusive human beings appearance up to and aspire to emulate. The majority people are encouraged thru what we see in magazines, in addition to what our pals and celebrities wear whilst locating out what to put in our closets. The diploma of delight we revel in is extensively decreased whilst we're exposed to classified ads encouraging us to place on t-shirts.

When you make bigger a better connection with a emblem, you emerge as extra emotionally worried in it. That method you may be interested by what they do subsequent and revel in like you have were given a stake of their success. This improves the opportunity that you can interact with their postings and trust what they've got to mention.

Another cause for its recognition is that people experience reliving the memories of others. Sharing details about special human beings's lives may want to make your private social media debts greater exciting and appealing to others.

When you use your personal name as your brand, but, you've got the potential to sell your "fee proposition," that's what makes maximum worthwhile devices promote. This is your "promise" to clients concerning the blessings that they'll collect from buying your product. The emotional hook you use and the manner of existence you want others to adopt are both vital factors of your argument.

The 3 C's of Influencers

Will you boom your efforts at persuading others? Do you motive to be maximum of the nice to your area, attracting the most ideal sponsors? The subsequent step is to be aware about THE THREE C's.

Content

The key to being an influencer is developing great content. It might no longer count wide variety whether you use Tik Tok, YouTube, or Instagram. People watch to be inspired, knowledgeable, or amused, and your cloth fulfills their goals.

This is crucial for networking, getting mentions from influential human beings, and finding sponsors. More people will want to be related collectively collectively together with your emblem due to the increased exquisite of your content fabric material. We'll pass right into a manner to carry out all of those later in the ebook.

So how can you deliver superb content material? It all comes all the manner right down to reevaluating your charge proposition. You need to understand the motivations within the once more of and advantages that your goal market expects from supporting you. After you've got it down, you'll be capable of use that emotional hook to preserve drawing them in.

Another vital detail of creating remarkable content material cloth fabric is to be actual and actual to your self. Your purpose marketplace will apprehend your honesty and sincerity and could hook up with you on a deeper degree. It is also crucial to live up to date with modern trends and topics for your region of hobby and create content material that is each well timed and relevant. You can also collaborate with exceptional influencers to create even higher content material that appeals to a much broader purpose market.

Community

For influencers, participation in the community is important. The key time period right here is "social," because of the fact they may be social networks.

In wonderful phrases, communication is the motive of those systems. You aren't effectively the use of the channels if you provide material however do not solution questions or comments.

Responding to questions from your target market will assist them experience more cushty and extra like they realise you. True "enthusiasts" are individuals who participate within the community surrounding your channel, in choice to passive site visitors. The "smooth sell" method is a powerful device inside the palms of a person of have an effect on. Imagine the fee of your life schooling at 2,000 € consistent with session. Using snap shots of yourself having an exquisite time, you subtly sell it which you provide lifestyles training. People will come to you with inquiries, and you'll need to decide if you may assist them out after speaking to them. The next step is to speak about the pricing and information of this machine in advance than signing any contracts. If you're an influencer, this could assist you promote real "excessive-rate price ticket" objects.

Additionally, website hosting live Q&A sessions, giveaways, and specific interactive activities can assist boom engagement and deliver a lift in your courting at the side of your aim market.

Connection

The very last step is to attach. Collaboration with distinct important influencers in your agency will provide you an advantage and help you upward push to the pinnacle extra quick. Success as an influencer is as lots approximately who you recognize as it's far about what you apprehend.

If you hyperlink yourself with the groups that clients adore, you will locate success as well. To trap such sponsors, you have to promote yourself, of direction. Don't sincerely sit down down there and desire that they may come to you.

How do you interact along with your coworkers? One preference is to join our personal membership of creative kinds.

However, it is crucial to be selective whilst selecting who to collaborate with and to handiest paintings with producers that align together with your values and ideals. Building sturdy relationships with awesome influencers and brands can also cause future possibilities and collaborations. Networking is likewise essential in growing your affect. Attend activities and conferences for your area of hobby and connect with different corporation experts. This will let you live updated with the present day day tendencies and advantage treasured insights into the enterprise organization.

This e-book will cover all of those subjects tremendous through a methodical development of sections. If you examine those steps cautiously, you may increase right right into a powerful influence.

Chapter 10: The Importance of Analytics

Analytics are critical for any influencer who desires to develop their logo and attain a miles broader target audience. By tracking your standard performance metrics, you can advantage insights into what is running and what isn't, and regulate your method ultimately. This records can assist you switch out to be privy to tendencies, styles, and regions for development for your content fabric, engagement, and fundamental performance.

Some essential metrics to music consist of your audience demographics, engagement charges, acquire and impressions, and net web site web site traffic. You can use equipment like Google Analytics, social media analytics, and influencer advertising platforms to degree and take a look at those metrics.

By regularly reviewing your analytics, you may moreover degree the achievement of your campaigns and collaborations, and determine which ones are generating the excellent consequences. This facts can help you make extra knowledgeable picks approximately your partnerships and content material cloth material creation transferring ahead.

Additionally, analytics allow you to stay aggressive in a crowded influencer place. By keeping a watch to your competition' overall performance metrics, you could discover what's strolling for them and doubtlessly adapt the ones strategies to your very non-public emblem.

Overall, analytics provide valuable insights that could tell and improve your influencer approach, supporting you stay in advance of the curve and collect your desires.

Choosing Your Niche

The desire of marketplace area of interest is a vital one even as launching a net web page or social media platform. Your preference could have an effect on the kind of material you embody, the layout and fashion of your internet site, further to the aim marketplace and visitor types you can cope with.

There are numerous additives worried in this selection, and we can glaringly base our preference on what we assume could probably result in earnings. So, we are able to pick out a part of the marketplace this is both famous and not too complete of competition.

Nevertheless, in case you rely certainly on seek engine advertising and area performance, you can in all likelihood make a lousy desire and select out out a topic that doesn't art work with either. This phase will communicate why addressing a few topics on your net website is probably a terrible concept, and how doing so can also want to become costing you numerous cash.

For example, you may choose a subject this is too large or too slender, making it difficult to attract the right intention marketplace. Additionally, you could choose out a topic this is too debatable or polarizing, that can turn off capacity clients and harm your logo reputation.

Consider era. Since you are searching out a method on line, you glaringly have an hobby in technology, so deciding on this as your specialty sounds sensible, proper? No way, now not if you want to construct a large hardware-centric technology website. Why? Because you could want get proper of entry to to all of the contemporary era and gadgets as they become to be had to investigate them and take appealing snap shots of them at the way to compete with massive web sites. I've come across some distance too many tech net sites that observe one smartphone after which wonder why they do not get masses website site visitors. Furthermore, comparable internet internet web sites will submit breaking data in that corporation as fast as it will become available. They can be capable of offer you with technical statistics for a brand new product a long manner quicker than a one-guy internet website online, making your tech internet website on-line absolutely vain.

You can get press releases and invites to exchange shows and specific sports with the useful resource of the usage of those web sites. Your net web page could in no way be the first-class due to the truth there can be no manner you can release with that degree of get right of entry to.

If you launch a comedian ebook internet site, you will want to shop for each comedian e-book every month, similarly to preserve up with everything the teams do and get interviews. Following that, undergo every one.

To further increase on the challenge of choosing your place of interest, it's far important to be aware that it have to additionally align together with your hobbies and expertise. If you select a spot definitely based mostly on earnings ability without considering your ardour and records inside the place, you can end up burning out fast or losing interest in growing content material material. Additionally, it's far crucial to behavior thorough studies and evaluation of the marketplace and goal marketplace in your preferred niche. This consists of identifying the competition, records the target audience's desires and alternatives, and studying developments and patterns within the enterprise. Another vital element to consider is the scalability of your area of interest. While it's far essential to begin with a particular and targeted region of interest, you need to additionally don't forget the capacity for growth and enlargement within the destiny. This includes exploring associated topics and sub-niches that could attraction to a much broader target audience without straying too far out of your middle recognition. It's moreover important to hold in thoughts the durability of your chosen vicinity of interest. Will it remain relevant and in name for within the long time, or is it a passing fashion at the manner to rapid lose its enchantment? Conducting thorough studies and evaluation will allow you to make a extra informed choice. Overall, choosing your area of interest is a important preference that requires careful hobby and making plans. By taking the time to find out a worthwhile, relevant, and sustainable place of hobby that aligns collectively collectively together with your pursuits and expertise, you could set your self up for lengthy-time period achievement as a content cloth creator or influencer.

The Response Against Oversaturation

That does not suggest that you could never be able to write about technology or every different difficulty this is fast developing; all it implies is that you need to take heed to your limitations and reputation on what's maximum vital to you.

You might be capable of avoid the troubles described above if, instead of writing approximately "technology," you stated "e-video video video games" or "The crowdfunding platform" Instead, bypass for a subject like food that doesn't require regular revisions to mirror the maximum today's findings; this may prevent time and electricity. By doing so, you can have the capacity to offer "evergreen content cloth fabric."

If you keep in mind a effective location internal a forte, you will be in a role to speak with a much extra unique shape of people. Since you'll be speaking straight away to them, you'll have a smaller goal market, however that focus on market may be a long way extra engaged. Since you may be capable of use the "pass-to marketplace" approach, you may have a much much much less tough time communicating together with your target market (Find out how they spend their time and what they do) in addition to the truth that you will have a higher knowledge of a way to create something so that you can attraction to your "client man or woman" (aim marketplace).

Choose a niche this is greater tailored on your pastimes than one this is massive. Then decide on one on the way to permit you to deal with a fantastic agency of people.

In addition, it is vital to hold in mind that selecting an opening which you're passionate about will make the whole device greater exciting and fun. If you want cooking, for instance, developing content material fabric about food will experience lots less like paintings and more like a amusing interest. This enthusiasm may even shine through to your content cloth, making it more attractive to your aim market. Another method to combat oversaturation is to technique the topic from a completely specific perspective. For example, in choice to growing however another fashion blog, you may attention on sustainable style or vintage apparel. This way, you could differentiate yourself from the opposition and appeal to a more unique, region of interest target audience. It's also essential to maintain in thoughts of your target audience's needs and options. Conducting studies and gathering remarks out of your target audience assist you to create content material fabric that is greater relevant and treasured to them. This can bring about better engagement and a extra dependable following. Finally, it's miles vital to be affected man or woman and steady in building your area of interest. It takes effort and time to set up your self as an authority in a particular area, but with willpower and perseverance, you may create a successful niche platform that resonates together along with your audience.

Picking a Niche That Excites You

A piece of recommendation: ensure to choose a area of understanding that you have previous information in, are obsessed with, and absolutely understand. One of the satisfactory mistakes that businesses and those who "want to" be influential might also make is choosing subjects that they do not surely apprehend or have a stake in. This can occur very regularly.

Those who aren't knowledgeable about or interested in sports activities regularly lease a creator to put in writing about it for them, and the author they rent is also a general author who does not have any revel in in sports activities activities activities, with the hope that the issue would possibly advantage fulfillment. This is a fairly commonplace state of affairs.

To begin with, you can't obtain success as an influencer except you stay the way you teach and suggest.

Nobody desires to observe a cosmetics and beauty influencer who could no longer use makeup or a fitness influencer who's overweight and out of form.

Not simplest that, however the superb of the statistics is constantly a good deal higher while the author or writer is aware and cares about the issue.

The actual thriller to being influential is that this. You need to first installation yourself as a idea leader in order to steer others. This is the right key to having a large effect. In order to steer particular people, you want to first set up your self as a idea leader to your situation. This method that your message want to be intriguing, idea-scary, and compelling.

If a author does no longer actually apprehend the fitness place of hobby, they may write about the way to get abs and massive biceps. These are clearly distinct difficulty subjects which have been written approximately severa instances on numerous net websites. To located it genuinely, this isn't sufficient to herald a big institution of involved humans.

If the author depended on vintage property, it's miles even much more likely that they may be ignorant of the maximum state-of-the-art inclinations and dispositions in the health and health employer.

On the opportunity hand, writing on a topic from the perspective of a person who's acquainted with it and appreciates it will result in the manufacturing of content material material that is authentic, tough, and beneficial to exclusive people who are acquainted with and similar to the situation matter. This is the way you decorate the range of human beings following you.

Create a Logo and a Mission Statement

The next step is to provide you a brand venture declaration and brand. You have selected your vicinity of understanding and narrowed it to a positive trouble of view as a way to supply it a completely particular and private spin that is special to you. The best thing that stays is to increase a emblem throughout the idea in query.

You are the brand, so there may be no want to don't forget a name in your business corporation (possibly). But you have to furthermore remember developing a task announcement.

A challenge announcement expresses an purpose. Your content material fabric's cause and message is probably clarified as a forestall quit end result. What precisely are you in search of to speak? Your content cloth's aim and message may be clarified as a quit end result. What exactly are you trying to talk? To whom are you talking? Why is that, then?

Because of this, there might be a huge difference in how you'll promote it yourself, promote yourself, and whom you will cause. Because of this, your "price proposition" may even exchange. This is the manner of existence you promote and offer, and those are the forms of blessings someone ought to get from copying and adapting your conduct.

Then, this should be validated to your brand. So, your logo, or at the least, the way your internet internet site and social media payments are designed, ought to display this. If you control your brand properly, anybody who visits your net web web page or social media account should have the capability to tell proper away if the belongings you percentage are suitable for them.

When growing a emblem, preserve in mind that it should be clean, memorable, and visually attractive. Your logo may be a example of your emblem, so it should successfully bring your logo's challenge and values. It must moreover be bendy enough for use in the course of all of your advertising substances. Your venture assertion and brand want to be consistent together in conjunction with your emblem's tone and messaging. If your logo is greater crucial and expert, then your logo and assignment declaration should replicate that. If your emblem is greater lighthearted and humorous, then your emblem and undertaking statement have to mirror that as properly. Don't be afraid to get remarks from others ultimately of the layout device. Ask friends, own family, or maybe colleagues for their mind and opinions to your logo and task announcement. This permit you to select out out any regions for development and make certain that your emblem efficiently represents your message.

Chapter 11: Choose Your Platform after Deciding

Now which you recognize what you may write about, it is time to plot how you will write it In one among a type phrases, it relies upon on which platform you need exceptional and what form of content you need to make.

But preserving a blog and writing posts for it's far very one-of-a-kind from having a YouTube channel and making films for it. Which platform would be the best healthy for you?

The first detail you ought to apprehend is which you don't want to paste to at least one platform. For instance, I tell every body who has numerous have an impact at once to make a YouTube account. But you want to moreover have payments on Facebook, Instagram, Twitter, and YouTube. The more systems you have got got, the greater opportunities human beings will have to connect with you. Also, in case you are lively on some of social networking web sites, you may frequently show up in their records feeds.

As a forestall result, your intention market will recognize extra approximately you and your emblem, with a purpose to make them sense greater related to you and what you want to provide. Still, maximum artists will pick out out one "foremost" platform in which they will spend the maximum time and electricity to get the maximum enthusiasts and characteristic the most have an impact on.

The reaction may additionally rely upon the shape of emblem you need to collect and the kind of content cloth you need to percent. It additionally is predicated upon on what makes you experience the most relaxed. Visual advertising and marketing and advertising has sizable blessings for influencers. "A picture is virtually well worth a thousand phrases," due to the fact the saying is going, so posting a unmarried image on Instagram may be a much better manner to get your message in the course of or make humans revel in something than actually writing facts.

This works very well for topics that have photographs. This consists of things like paintings, splendor, and indoors layout. If your project count number is being profitable, you can display off suits and awesome products. This is a extraordinary manner to market a lifestyle.

It's crucial to keep in mind that authenticity is high on Instagram, so in case you're not absolutely dwelling the lifestyle you're promoting, it may be tough to hold lovers and engagement. Using relatable captions and speaking in your goal marketplace also can assist you build a robust community spherical your logo. Since it's far a form of seen verbal exchange, it is straightforward to make a big impact right away. It's additionally an extremely private platform, so that you should revel in comfortable speaking to the digital digital camera and with the way you appearance (more on this in an upcoming bankruptcy). Another problem to consider is how you can make these movies. They take heaps longer to make due to the reality you need to edit, separate the audio from the video, and so on. There are severa techniques to make the model extra scalable. For instance, in case you use your cellular phone to file greater motion photos and make your fashion extra "non-public," you will be able to make greater content faster. This could no longer normally appear, despite the fact that. If you may do all of those gadgets, YouTube is a fantastic location to get to apprehend your audience because of the reality you will be speakme right away to them and the use of song and enhancing to stress domestic the emotional factors. You can fast grow your goal marketplace if you make loads of unique content that makes a speciality of vicinity of hobby topics and key phrases that no one else is using. Influencers have a splendid greater alternative: they are capable of begin a weblog. This desire is proper for dad and mom that don't need to be on digital virtual digital camera as often or who need to speak about more "highbrow" topics. If you need to jot down down long essays or explainers and your trouble isn't very clear, a written approach may be lots higher.

Also, net websites paintings properly with a sizable sort of strategies to make cash. For instance, you can set up an internet preserve or hyperlink your internet website online on your exclusive social media debts simply so your sidebar suggests an Instagram or Twitter feed.

It's very easy to proportion your posts on social media. But making this form of content material takes a number of time, requires a few writing capabilities, and has a much a great deal less "instant" effect. But getting regarded thru a blog takes hundreds longer and is a tremendous deal extra hard due to the fact there is no "platform."

There are numerous extra websites to be had for influencers, which incorporates twitch, Twitter, and Tiktok. All of those possibilities, within the period in-between, are a good buy a whole lot less suitable for serving because the "number one" platform for one cause or a few different. Most of the time, the content material cloth fabric that is made is both very quick, very quick-lived, or perhaps live. Because of this, you can have less to offer sponsors and advertisers, on the manner to make it tougher in order to develop.

The Pros and Cons of Each Platform

As an influencer, it's far important to carefully evaluate the professionals and cons of every platform earlier than deciding on which of them to focus on. Here are a few execs and cons of the maximum famous structures for influencers:

Instagram

Pros:

Large purchaser base with over a thousand million month-to-month active customers

Highly visible platform, making it perfect for showcasing pics and films

High engagement costs in evaluation to specific structures

Offers numerous abilities together with memories and Reels to help you diversify your content material

Cons:

High opposition due to the huge quantity of influencers on the platform

Limited hyperlink sharing competencies, making it tough to electricity visitors to outside internet sites

Algorithm adjustments can notably impact visibility and achieve

YouTube

Pros:

Second biggest are seeking engine after Google, making it an super platform for content cloth cloth discovery

Longer-shape video content material material is greater drastically well-known on YouTube

High capability for monetization thru advertisements, sponsorships, and products profits

Strong community engagement and collaboration possibilities

Cons:

Requires tremendous investment in tool and manufacturing remarkable to create terrific movies

May take an extended time to collect an goal market and gain monetization as compared to other systems

Higher limitations to access for modern day creators due to the saturation of the platform

TikTok

Pros:

Huge growth capability because of the platform's popularity with greater younger audiences

Quick and easy content introduction with a whole lot of incorporated equipment and consequences

Algorithm favors new content material cloth creators, making it a whole lot less complex for contemporary day money owed to benefit visibility

Opportunity for viral content material and massive exposure

Cons:

May not be appropriate for all types of content material cloth or audiences

Limited monetization opportunities compared to big structures

May face elevated competition and saturation as greater influencers flock to the platform

Twitter

Pros:

High capacity for virality due to the platform's interest on actual-time updates and trending topics

Ideal for short-shape content material cloth fabric which includes expenses, mind, and opinions

Opportunity for engagement with a quite energetic and various purchaser base

Cons:

Limited seen capabilities as compared to special structures, making it masses much less suitable for visual content cloth creators

High frequency of tweets required to keep engagement ranges

Limited monetization possibilities compared to different systems

Facebook

Pros:

Large and severa purchaser base with a excessive functionality for acquire

Strong emphasis on community building and engagement

Highly customizable options for content material material fabric sharing and goal market targeting

Cons:

Decreasing herbal attain and engagement due to set of rules changes

May no longer be as popular among more younger audiences as compared to exceptional systems

Can be hard to build an target market because of the immoderate opposition from groups and distinctive influencers

Overall, it's miles critical to select a platform that aligns collectively along with your content fabric style, purpose marketplace, and desires as an influence. By cautiously comparing the professionals and cons of every platform, you may make an knowledgeable desire and maximize your functionality for achievement.

Chapter 12: Produce Content

The subsequent step is the maximum important: making content material material! What makes humans want to visit your internet site and examine you on social media? Due to the fact they need to have a laugh or check some component. Just how do you try this? Making use of content! Your internet site's content cloth is what is going to supply humans there and maintain them coming once more for added. The first-class way to make first rate content cloth is to make sure it allows people in a few manner. It's a first rate concept to keep asking yourself, "Would YOU observe this?"

Don't be afraid to expose off your personality and particular perspective to your content material. This is what gadgets you aside from others in your field and makes your content material stand out.

The pointers underneath will help you are making first-rate content fabric no matter what platform you use.

How to Write Blog Posts That People Can't Stop Reading

Do you need to put in writing articles that human beings find out thrilling, tough to vicinity down, and flow into them emotionally? Want to invest your phrases for your readers so you can promote greater and get extra human beings to click on for your links?

How you write for the net might be very unique from the manner you write for other audiences. Even even though the crucial regulations of English grammar do not trade, how you write will depend upon your reason and the situation in which you are writing. When you write on-line, you need to be as exciting as viable to capture and maintain a reader's hobby. You additionally want to put in writing in a way that builds reliable readers who're probable to click on on to your links and purchase eBooks or specific topics that your advertisers are selling.

You'll word that nicely-written weblog posts and net internet site on-line content cloth are written in a positive manner that draws the reader in and tells a story as you look at. It could now not simply let you know what it dreams to mention; it is also you with the aid of asking you rhetorical questions and describing a way of existence you may want to study. You will examine this thru time and revel in, but you moreover mght want to understand how humans think and experience.

When writing, keep topics concise and to the element. Nobody desires to study a prolonged, rambling piece that does not get to the heart of the problem. Finally, continually proofread your content material material earlier than publishing to ensure it is mistakes-free and expert.

A little psychology can flow an extended way towards making your readers very interested by what you have got were given to say and placing on on your every word. This is the manner to do it.

Be Honest and Straight

Writing immediately for your readers is the number one element you need to do if you want to seize their hobby and get them to pay interest. To make the visitor sense like they may be being talked to in desire to passively studying some thing, you need to use quite a few direct languages to cope with them. Use the phrase "you" often. This form of first-character writing is used.

Influencers are popular because of the truth they provide human beings a revel in of familiarity. You also can quietly evoke this mood through way of sincerely altering your writing fashion, as a manner to make you extensively extra convincing and compelling.

Also, you should keep in mind your readers' wants to hooked up writing right away to them.

Readers recognize writers who speak to them in a real way. Avoid using complex jargon or buzzwords that might turn off your target audience. Instead, preserve your writing clean and direct, and use language that resonates together together with your readers.

Think about the readers of your net website online, their hobbies, and their goals. Knowing this will help you write in a manner that engages your goal marketplace at the same time as moreover providing them with proper charge.

Describe a Story

When writing blog posts, keep in mind that "storytelling is search engine optimization for the human mind." In exceptional phrases, the human thoughts is built in a manner that makes it superb at know-how stories. Part of a tale framework is speakme about a subject out of your factor of view or the thing of view of someone .

This makes your content fabric hundreds greater exciting and allows your target marketplace get to understand you better, this is important for an influencer.

Additionally, incorporating non-public anecdotes and critiques can help to set up a reference to your readers and make your content material extra relatable. This can reason advanced engagement and a stronger following for your weblog.

Promote an Outcome

Your writing will ultimately "sell" a few thing to the reader. Writing is a brilliant method to speaking your thoughts to readers, whether you are looking for to promote a bodily product or truly a concept.

If you want your net internet web page to run well and deliver a few truely compelling studying cloth, you will need to make certain that every one of your posts are promoting approximately the identical factor. Each article may also moreover cover a severa mission rely, however they will all sell the idea that having a greater healthful body, a bigger financial group account, or a more fun sexual life is proper (this "final results" ought to fit what you understand approximately the patron). It is vital which you do no longer, beneath any instances, lose sight of the reason that people went for your internet site inside the first location.

Continue to tease the outcome of your articles and encourage your goal market to anticipate wherein your recommendation can also take them to hold them analyzing. Use persuasive language to recognition on the blessings of your product or concept, and show readers how it's going to decorate their lives

Write about your way of life so readers may additionally additionally furthermore see themselves in your characteristic. Finally, give them simply sufficient unique recommendation to cause them to experience like they'll be capable of be successful.

Become Passionate

Lastly, if you want people to take into account you, you need to be obsessed on what you're pronouncing and in fact accept as true with it. The best manner to get humans to shop for your ebook is to be so enthusiastic about it that it jumps off the page. Find your calling, do it nicely, after which use articles to sell the existence and feature you have made for your self.

Also, the proper way to use terms that make humans expect could have a massive impact. This word need to allow you to understand, "Hey, this is critical and could make a BIG difference on your lifestyles."

Using a tale structure, like I without a doubt defined, will assist your cloth soar. That term surely caught your interest.

To seize your audience's attention and make your idea pop off the web web page, be cautious no longer to grow to be overly emotional or lose sight of your number one goal.

Consistency is Key

Consistency is fundamental with reference to building a web presence as an influencer. This approach usually producing outstanding content material fabric and engaging along with your intention market on a regular basis. By doing so, you may set up yourself as a dependable supply of data and construct accept as true with at the side of your followers.

One of the maximum essential factors of consistency is maintaining a regular posting time table. This can variety depending at the platform you are the usage of, but it's vital to discover a time table that works for you and your target market. For instance, if you're a blogger, you could want to put up new content every week or two. If you are a YouTuber, you may want to put up motion images on a specific day of the week, like each Wednesday.

In addition to posting often, it's miles crucial to maintain consistency to your logo and messaging. This method the usage of the identical colorings, fonts, and format factors at some stage in all your structures, in addition to staying real on your area of hobby and private brand. This will assist to create a cohesive and recognizable image in your fanatics.

How to Create YouTube Videos With Professional and Interesting Material

With YouTube, you can come to be well-known with out ever having to stand a virtual digicam. You may moreover moreover completely distance yourself from the fabric by means of way of manner of putting in a channel with voiceovers and slide exhibitions, for instance. Of direction, as influencers, it isn't what we need to carry out. The significance of being seen talking in front of the digicam on the subjects we cowl close to constructing authority, accept as true with, and engagement can't be overstated.

That can be scary if you've in no way completed some factor adore it in advance than. To get began, bear in mind the following recommendation:

Having the Right Aura and Sound

If you want to begin a YouTube channel in order to be visible with the aid of pretty some human beings, make the excellent first impact you can through using the use of making some problem appealing, cute, and confident. This is vital in case you need to expose others a manner to act. Follow those policies to make certain it's the case.

How You Do Things

The manner you gift your mind is greater important than how you seem, and the aim is to be each precise, instructional, and expert at the same time as but together with that a laugh, "private" touch that will help you stand out and draw in the fans.

You need to strike a sensitive balance between scripted and authentic speech to try this. One strategy is to make a listing of the topics you need to speak about and region it inside the the the front of you on a board or in some different visible vicinity. Next, extra or lots less follow that listing, however be open to creating changes. Another tip is to upward thrust up at the same time as you speak. This will provide you with greater electricity and make you seem extra lively and exciting to splendid people. Gesticulation is proper, so permit it seem, however do now not push it or pay an excessive amount of hobby to it, for the motive that this might make it seem forced.

Last but now not least, it's far suitable to keep shooting regardless of what. Keep going so that you can discover a herbal rhythm and do not must forestall and start all of the time. When you are making a mistake, restart (leaving a wreck to facilitate modifying). Next, edit cautiously to get rid of as many pauses as viable even as keeping the story transferring fast and apparently. Don't worry in case you do not recognize this proper away. It takes time and workout.

A YouTube Content Strategy

A blog's content material material approach will probable be just like YouTube's. Insightful answers, strong arguments, and active participation in debate on a topic of hobby are all required. Try to preserve your trouble depend constant even as letting your individual shine thru in a way this is steady with the message of your enterprise enterprise enterprise.

It is critical to also bear in thoughts the visual detail of your content fabric, collectively with the use of great photographs and pictures. Using comments and social media to interact collectively with your target market also can assist construct a network round your content. Optimizing your content cloth cloth era is one of the maximum vital YouTube factors. It might be hard to supply multiple video each few weeks if you create 10-minute films which is probably closely edited and function an entire lot of stock material and tune. You need to instead discover ways to accelerate the content fabric creation device, which encompass supplying quick hints that high-quality remaining a couple of minutes or filming the "herbal speak" at the occasion after which uploading it in your cellular telephone.

Important YouTube rating parameters for video discovery

When figuring out wherein films will display up in are looking for effects, the set of policies that YouTube uses considers many special tendencies. The maximum vital factors are as follows:

1) Description, key phrases, and category for the video The identify, description, and tags of your films will decide how outcomes human beings can locate them at the same time as looking online.

2) Audience retention If you can maintain visitors looking your video for an extended duration, YouTube will provide it extra weight. YouTube's goal is to keep customers at the platform so long as possible. It's crucial to don't forget the manner to make your video content material exciting as a cease cease result.

The Best Ways to Make Amazing Instagram Posts

There are some factors to consider if you need to deliver fantastic Instagram content material. The first element people will word is the way you upload price. You have crucial options right right here: make visuals which can be thrilling, inspiring, or motivating, or write a textual content that is informative and beneficial (you could do each).

Think approximately how you could decorate your art work and make it appearance higher so that you can make pics which might be inspiring and motivating.

You ought to recognition on giving recommendation and thoughts, specially internal your description, if you need to generate cloth this is educational or offers charge thru know-how. By doing matters on this way, you deliver human beings a cause to assist and comply with you.

The first-rate manner to do it's miles to apply every. A splendor influencer must publish a photograph of herself shopping for at the equal time as sporting lovable makeup and searching perfect. This is every motivating and provoking for folks that need to look and experience like that. They must do that to get mind and have a look at more approximately beauty.

Don't be afraid to check with precise put up formats, along side carousels, movies, and reels. Each format has its very own precise benefits, and mixing matters up can assist keep your content cloth fabric sparkling and engaging. You can also use Instagram's numerous modifying device to feature filters, adjust brightness and assessment, and make different tweaks on your images and movies. If you want to gather a strong following on Instagram, you need to be posting often and on the right instances. Use Instagram analytics to decide while your fans are maximum active and try to schedule your posts because of this. You also can use gear to schedule your posts earlier, so you do no longer need to fear about manually posting each day.

Capturing Amazing Pictures

Another recommendation is to shoot pinnacle-notch pix. While it isn't vital, a first rate digicam might be quite useful.

Understanding composition and framing is pretty vital. The extraordinary pix must inform a tale, so do no longer take photos of the challenge right now. Instead, cognizance on a few thing related to or harking back to the problem.

One important issue of taking pix notable snap shots is choosing the proper location. Look for stimulating backgrounds, specific structure, or herbal landscapes that could feature a backdrop to your photographs. You can also try to find out places which might be plenty much less crowded to keep away from distractions and make it much less hard to get the ideal shot.

Think approximately the various strategies you'll in all likelihood deliver duration and tone. Altering the perspective of the image also can create scale, and lighting could have an impact on mood (and as a end end result importance).

Another tip is to be aware of the info. Look for stimulating patterns, textures, and sunglasses that might add visual interest on your pix. You also can test with one of a kind angles and perspectives to create a extra dynamic composition.

Consider the the the front, the middle ground, and the again at the equal time as you're looking to create mind-set for your images. Furthermore, do not forget the lighting fixtures, specially how attractive or unattractive it's far going to be, further to whether or now not or no longer or now not it's going to create first rate shadows.

When it involves enhancing your pix, a brilliant deal an awful lot less is frequently greater. Avoid going overboard with filters and adjustments, as this will make your photographs appearance synthetic and detract from their natural beauty. Instead, attention on subtle tweaks that enhance the prevailing shades and assessment.

As an influencer, it is your challenge to discover about things like seo, key-phrase studies, persuasive writing, net page optimization, the right style of posts, the super times to position up, the system to use, and exclusive comparable subjects. But in case you preserve reading as you flow, each put up you write will do better than the only in advance than it.

Finally, do now not be afraid to take dangers and attempt some thing new. Some of the most exciting and noteworthy pictures are people who ruin the rules and take a clean approach. By experimenting with outstanding techniques and patterns, you can enlarge your very personal specific voice and style as a photographer.

Chapter 13: Engage Your Followers

The subsequent crucial degree in your influencer industrial organisation approach is to have interaction your target market. This involves building an extended-lasting connection with your reason marketplace, in preference to definitely having them observe your weblog and comply with you on social media, to guide them to sense engaged and concerned in what you are doing.

The first and most apparent method for uplifting a collection of human beings is to engage with them, responding to comments published, in addition to to emails, direct messages, and unique kinds of conversation.

One of the worst topics you could do in your popularity is to ignore them because it appears as if you do not care approximately or are not interested in your target market.

By speaking to people, you open up a manner for them to speak to you and reason them to experience like they apprehend you. Spend a while to your responses, due to the fact even one must advocate loads to the proper person.

If you do no longer get many responses for your content material material on the start, it is able to be because of the reality you probably did no longer attain sufficient humans. In this situation, you need to get as many human beings involved as feasible. This can be finished short thru asking human beings to go away feedback on your movies and blogs. YouTube best helps you to talk to the virtual digicam, but Instagram has plenty of stickers that you may use to get humans to have interaction.

Get your target market to help or participate in a few place of the improvement of your profile. One of the best strategies to steer others to have interaction with you as an influencer is to apply this approach. Provide them with the choice to vote on the following fabric or to suggest names and wonderful components instead. As an immediate stop end result of this, they now have the effect that they have a stake inside the brand. Although this can appear to be a setback, the reality is that it certainly will increase the quantity of emotional connection and engagement.

Multiple Media & Cross-platform advertising

Keep in thoughts that tremendous communique channels and media lend themselves to building honest rapport with an target audience considerably more than others. Stories and live video artwork very well.

You can display your lovers what's going on behind the scenes through telling tales about your day and lifestyles. They also may be used to make polls, ask questions, and do different topics. On the alternative hand, live video facilitates you to speak to and respond for your aim market proper away. It's a outstanding manner for them to be curious and for you to reveal that you're a actual person at the same time. Use this to show off your talents on specific sports or just to talk to the virtual digital camera even as you're consuming lunch.

When the use of more than one media, it is vital to maintain in mind that every kind of media has its very very own specific strengths and weaknesses. For instance, whilst memories are first rate for giving followers a glimpse into your each day existence, live movies allow for actual-time interaction and engagement. Additionally, ensure that the media you select is relevant for your brand and the message you need to supply.

To successfully promote your content material cloth in some unspecified time in the future of more than one structures, it's far vital to tailor your method to each platform. Each platform has its very very very own precise audience, capabilities, and content cloth codecs. For example, the manner you promote your content material fabric on Instagram can be outstanding than the manner you sell it on Twitter or LinkedIn. It's essential to understand the nuances of every platform and adjust your technique as a give up result.

The benefits of move-platform promoting are severa. First, it allows you to attain a wider purpose marketplace. By selling your content material cloth cloth on a couple of systems, you boom the opportunities of accomplishing individuals who won't have discovered you otherwise. Second, it lets in to decorate your brand during one-of-a-type systems. By commonly promoting your content material fabric cloth in the course of a couple of platforms, you set up a more potent logo identity and increase logo reputation.

Overall, bypass-platform merchandising is an crucial method for influencers who want to maximise their attain and impact. By selling your content material material fabric in some unspecified time in the future of multiple systems, you may boom your purpose market, help your brand identification, and improve your attempting to find engine ratings.

Participating within the Community

Making connections to your place of understanding elsewhere is a few other way to begin building your first community. Being active on a well-known discussion board or exceptional structures to your region have to have a huge effect on how properly your emblem is idea and how reliable your clients are.

When it includes constructing a community round your brand, being energetic on popular forums or distinctive online structures on your concern may be mainly powerful. By participating in discussions and presenting beneficial recommendation, you could set up yourself as an authority on your location of interest and appeal to new enthusiasts to your logo. It's critical to recollect that constructing a community takes effort and time, however the rewards can be fantastic. By connecting with like-minded humans and contributing to the verbal exchange, you could create a devoted following so that you can assist develop your emblem.

Networking and Collaboration

Networking is an vital part of constructing a a success profession, and it is no remarkable with regards to becoming an influencer. One of the number one steps to becoming an influencer is to penetrate the circle of influencers in your niche. This may be achieved with the useful resource of attending occasions, connecting with others on social media, and carrying out out to influencers on your place. By building relationships with others for your business enterprise, you can collaborate on initiatives, take a look at from every one-of-a-type's testimonies, or perhaps increase your attain by tapping into each unique's audiences.

You need to first penetrate that circle in case you want to development as an influencer. Here is some strong recommendation to get you going.

How and why need to an influencer community?

The significance of networking can't be overstated, specially inside the worldwide of influencers. Although a variety of us aren't in reality outgoing, growing the right connections can cause success. Working from domestic may have appeared like the ideal answer for loads, however the reality is that achieving out to coworkers or organization companions is regularly critical for advancement.

Starting small is excessive in phrases of networking. It is nearly not feasible to gather a reaction from pinnacle game enthusiasts within the company, so it's essential initially competitors who are at some point of the same duration as your modern-day-day identity. Collaborating with others thru move-promotional sports is a great manner to double the variety of your fanatics and paintings your manner up the ladder.

For instance, if you have 5,000 Instagram fanatics, partnering with every exclusive creator who has the same range of fanatics can motive mutual advantages. You can carry out a shout-out with every unique and benefit 500 enthusiasts whenever. By repeating this technique with particular creators, you can attain 10,000 fans rapid, making it less tough to target massive influencers.

One of the simplest strategies to growth visibility and connections as a blogger is thru vacationer jogging a weblog. By contributing content to particular blogs, you may set up yourself as a concept leader in your industry and gain exposure to a far broader target market.

Additionally, connecting with human beings in person is important for leaving a long-lasting impact. Attending networking activities is a brilliant way to satisfy new people and strike up a verbal exchange. If you cannot get to apprehend them at an event, hold in thoughts hiring them for a mission. This way, they ought to touch you and you may set up a connection.

It's important to preserve in touch together along with your contacts, but be respectful in their time. If they do no longer respond in your first message, try commenting on some of their posts earlier than sending some other message. Remember, influencers get busier as their fan base expands, but that doesn't mean they're no longer interested in what you have to mention. By continuing to have interaction with them, you may installation a valuable courting.

Chapter 14: The Influence of Habits

Everything you understand a way to do now, you determined. Think approximately that momentarily after which don't forget the number one detail you possibly did on the same time as mountaineering away from bed this morning. What has become it? Can you do not forget? Whether you may or can't, the reality is which you did something you probably did without thinking about it.

You can do one million topics once you wake up, and there's a excessive threat you do the same thing every day. Doing something usually like that's what makes it a dependency.

Habits are sports and behaviors repeated constantly and may manifest consciously or subconsciously. From nail biting, it truly is often unconscious, to brushing your tooth two times every day, finished intentionally, we're all creatures of addiction, and also you aren't exempted.

Habits can appear consciously or unconsciously, and now and again it could be each. Footballers have been kicking the ball due to the fact they're 6 or 7; some even begin kicking in advance than they will be five. They try this continuously every day till they end up experts.

In their scenario, this addiction is decided out, because of this that you could examine genuine behavior as lots as terrible behavior. Both have a giant effect to your life.

Impact of Habits

The international has billions of conduct, and every ought to have an impact on you and people round you. It is crucial to have a examine that a dependancy isn't most effective shaped at the same time as you do something whilst you don't perform a bit issue as well. It may be a addiction. Someone can say, "Oh! Jack has a addiction of now not cleansing his room." Doing a few issue is a addiction as plenty as doing no longer some thing is likewise a dependancy.

Habits can appreciably have an effect in your existence. It can improve your physical fitness or become worse it.

Habits can enhance your social lifestyles or spoil it. It can enhance your monetary lifestyles and mental health but moreover destroy it. It all relies upon on what conduct you have.

Some human beings begin their day with coffee and then skip directly to exercising. Some start their day with smoke and alcohol. One is ideal for physical health, while the alternative is volatile.

We all have conduct we take delight in, however our approach is fantastic, which plays a role in how we increase in existence.

Habits can help us have an effect on our existence and that of others spherical us.

Influence is the capacity to get your self or others to do what you need.

A footballer wishes the ball in the decrease again of the net, a basketball participant dreams the ball to undergo the ring, and a guitarist goals the solo on a track to sound beautiful and captivating. What do all of them do? They exercise and exercising a few extra till it all will become a addiction, 2nd nature, a few aspect they may be able to do without considering.

These people have observed to steer themselves to do the stupid stuff that has large rewards. However, have an impact on doesn't prevent with your self. You also can have an impact on people to get what you want; getting to know excellent and healthful behavior is a way to get there.

The Importance of Influence

The benefits of have an effect on are numerous. The following are some advantages of have an impact on;

1.   It let you bring together relationships with people. They might be mentors or really someone you admire.

2.   It allow you to obtain the goals you've set for your self.

3.   It ought to make you an powerful and appropriate chief.

4.   It allow you to get earlier in any profession you choose

five.   It could boom your danger of achievement in whatever you select

To have an impact on yourself and others, you want to make bigger competencies to help you try this.

Communication abilities and stress tolerance bypass an prolonged way in helping you grow to be influential to your self and the humans round you.

Chapter 15: Building Strong Relationships

Relationships are the middle of each society and the rare glue that holds the arena together. One manner or every special, we're in a courting with severa human beings, in case you want to preserve for a long term.

Relationships carry love, affection, intimacy, and every so often, hate. All of those may be motivations to emerge as higher.

Habits for Building Strong Relationships

Habit 1: Active Listening and Empathy

The first step in influencing people is constructing a courting with them. You can't affect who you don't recognize. You want to apprehend them, and the super manner to do that is through energetic listening and empathy.

Active listening lets in you to have a have a look at them and gain their consider. Active listening is more than taking note of phrases. It consists of your body language, your gestures, connecting with what they will be sharing, and being really engaged in what they're sharing. It consists of getting rid of every distraction that can be a barrier to the communication.

How can you exercise the dependancy of lively listening?

1.   Practice retaining eye touch: Looking into a person's eyes as they talk to you conveys interest and admire for them.

2.   Restrain your self from interrupting: expect them to in reality particular themselves in advance than responding. Don't interrupt or attempt to anticipate what they are attempting to say.

three. Employ non-verbal cues: Make gestures consisting of smiling, nodding, and mildly mirroring their frame language as they communicate. All the ones non-verbal cues display the speaker that you are paying attention and without a doubt engaged in what they're announcing.

four. Ask inquiries to clarify: that is often underemphasized. When someone speaks, and you don't have a question, they often sense like you aren't listening. Practice this via the use of the use of listening cautiously and asking the speaker questions that could lead them to make clear what they've stated. This can be a remarkable device addiction in the observe room or while meeting a mentor.

5. Reflect on the communique and paraphrase: This is a wonderful way to recognize what to invite. Quickly mirror on what this man or woman has said, summarize what you heard, and then ask questions for explanation.

These five steps are wholesome verbal exchange behavior that you may examine. The direct opposites of these behavior are interruption, avoiding eye contact, and closed frame language, due to this which you are bored of the conversation and would really like to escape.

So, examine these conduct consciously with the resource of mentally noting those hints even as talking. After every day, you can moreover ask your self questions based totally definitely mostly on these behavior.

The first detail to do each time you need to begin a verbal exchange is to eliminate distractions, which includes your cell smartphone, stopping the track, or some thing you are doing that might motive distractions.

Habit 2: Effective Communication Skills

Effective verbal exchange is an crucial lifestyles expertise. You want to talk to human beings if you want to persuade them. That is the first-class way; if you can't speak efficaciously, you could discover it difficult to get many stuff finished.

Effective conversation doesn't stop with talking or expressing your feelings, it's miles extra than that; it entails listening, too. That is why, to comprehend effective communique, the number one dependancy you want to increase is energetic listening. We've finished that earlier, now to the opportunity steps.

1.   Clarity and conciseness: Do you want to say no a party invitation? Some people use half of of the phrases in the dictionary to say no. A easy "no, I received't be going to the celebration with you" is all you want. It is obvious and concise. Practice doing this greater often, and you may get your message for the duration of without strain. By all approach, keep away from the usage of jargon and buzzwords. Your reason is to ship a message, so cast off the entirety that doesn't make a contribution to that message.

2.   Use your frame language to speak: Are you happy about some thing? Smile and provide an open frame gesture. Depending at the form of verbal exchange, constantly use your non-verbal cues. Avoid crossing your fingers across your body, making you appear shielding. Be assured.

three. Show empathy: Is your buddy having a lousy day? Don't pile on it. Show empathy. Put yourself in their shoes and apprehend what they're going through. When they percentage their challenges with you, don't decide them. Acknowledge their feeling and assist them via it.

4.   Ask questions: it shows your interest in the conversation, and they want to tell you extra.

Habit three: Trust and Authenticity

To turn out to be a person of have an effect on, you want don't forget to have folks who consider you sufficient to do what you need. To try this, you need to be real, and also you want to be a person of your word.

Authenticity comes from expertise your self and furthermore being obvious in the whole component you do. No one trusts the shady individual. Be enterprise in showing yourself, sharing what you have got have been given and apprehend, and embracing vulnerability.

Show your emotions. Let humans see who you're and what makes you tick. And from there, you could gather take into account with the useful resource of,

1. Keeping guarantees: I need to assume there's a believe meter, and on every occasion you hold a promise you made, this meter will growth. When you break guarantees, but, you are decreasing people's recall.

2. Listening actively and continuously: When you take notice of humans without judging, they mark you as honest because of the truth you are not stimulated with the useful resource of a few issue aside from doing the proper element. It's all about receive as actual with; being a high-quality listener takes you a step nearer.

Chapter 16: Building Confidence

Confidence is critical in influencing humans. Imagine a trendy about to visit battle fidgeting in the presence of his infantrymen. That's now not smooth to anticipate if you are one of the squaddies.

However, each preferred is confident and suggests it without even attempting. Do you apprehend why? They don't have blind self notion, which is what breeds ego. Their self guarantee comes from their achievements; the evidence is the celebrities on their shoulder and stripes on their chest.

If you want to gather self assurance, you ought to draw close those behavior.

Habits to Build Confidence

Habits four: Set Actionable Goals and artwork to acquire them.

Actionable desires are goals you could paintings on, not indistinct fantasies.

To set actionable desires, you need to hire the SMART approach, which makes the dreams a good deal less tough to art work on and attain.

S-Specific: Make sure the desires you area are precise. Like powerful conversation, make sure your goals are clean. For example, don't say I want to jot down down a e-book sooner or later; it is not precise enough. Instead, say, "I need to write my ebook – the way to play football with out stress – through ensuring I write a financial disaster each day."

M-Measurable: Your desires should be measurable. If no longer, you received't be capable of music your improvement. For the example above, you may with out troubles degree the e-book writing intention because of the truth you already stated you need to write down down a bankruptcy every day. There are seven days in line with week, so if you take a look at your manuscript, you may find out if you left out a day.

www.ingramcontent.com/pod-product-compliance
Lightning Source LLC
Chambersburg PA
CBHW071122050326
40690CB00008B/1305